# ANOTHER WORLD'S ZOMBIE APOCALYPSE IS *NOT* MY PROBLEM!

BY Haru Yayari   ILLUSTRATED BY Fuyuki

Another World's Zombie Apocalypse Is Not My Problem!
Haru Yayari

Translation by Charis Messier

Illustration by Fuyuki
Title Design by KC Fabellon
Editing by Nicole Brugger-Dethmers
Proofreading & Book Design by A.M. Perrone

This book is a work of fiction. Names, characters, businesses, places, events and incidents are either the products of the author's imagination or used in a fictitious manner. Any resemblance to actual events, locales, or persons, living or dead, is purely coincidental.

Another World's Zombie Apocalypse Is Not My Problem!
© 2016 by Haru Yayari
English translation rights reserved by
Cross Infinite World.

English translation ©2019 Cross Infinite World

All rights reserved. In accordance with U.S. Copyright Act of 1976, no part of this publication may be reproduced, distributed, or transmitted in any form or by any means, including photocopying, recording, or other electronic or mechanical methods, without the prior written permission of the publisher, except in the case of brief quotations embodied in critical reviews and certain other noncommercial uses permitted by copyright law. For permission requests, email the publisher, addressed "Attention: Permissions Coordinator," at the email below.

Cross Infinite World
contact@crossinfworld.com
www.crossinfworld.com

Published in the United States of America

Visit us at www.crossinfworld.com
Facebook.com/crossinfworld
Twitter.com/crossinfworld
crossinfiniteworld.tumblr.com

First Print Edition: September 2019

ISBN-10: 1-945341-40-8
ISBN-13: 978-1-945341-40-3

# TABLE OF CONTENTS

◆Chapter 1: Where Am I? — Pg 7
◆Chapter 2: Just When I Thought I Figured It Out… — Pg 13
◆Chapter 3: Apparently, Small Zombies Exist Too — Pg 21
◆Chapter 4: Grantz Kingdom — Pg 37
◆Chapter 5: The Reigning King of Charges — Pg 50
◆Chapter 6: The Holy Priestess of Spit — Pg 57
◆Chapter 7: The Zombies Are Serious Now — Pg 66
◆Chapter 8: Humans Are More Worrying Than Zombies — Pg 75
◆Chapter 9: A Reliable Little Scholar — Pg 82
◆Chapter 10: The Key to Ridding Exhaustion — Pg 91
◆Chapter 11: Hi, I'm Boss Lady — Pg 99
◆Chapter 12: Whenever Things Start to Go Well — Pg 107
◆Chapter 13: Boneless Ham — Pg 113
◆Chapter 14: Apparently, This Is What Happens… — Pg 121
◆Chapter 15: Signs of a Way Home — Pg 128
◆Chapter 16: My Goddess — Pg 137
◆Chapter 17: Believer Coalescence — Pg 144
◆Chapter 18: Handshake Sessions and Ardent Fans — Pg 154
◆Chapter 19: Separation and Reunion — Pg 162
◆Chapter 20: The Number-One Person I Don't Want to See… — Pg 174
◆Chapter 21: Quest to Vanquish the Dark Djinn — Pg 180
◆Chapter 22: Divine Punishment! — Pg 190
◆Chapter 23: The Real One Appears — Pg 195
◆Chapter 24: A Lot Has Happened — Pg 202
◆Chapter 25: Even a Zombie-Filled World Can Be Good — Pg 207
◆Epilogue: In a Wonderful World — Pg 213
◆After Story — Pg 221
◆Afterword — Pg 227

**Another World's Zombie Apocalypse Is Not My Problem!**

## ◆Chapter 1: Where Am I?

"IT reeks…!"

My name is Mizuha Kusunoki. I just woke up, and I already feel like crying. Tears have actually formed in my eyes and are threatening to tumble over.

These aren't tears produced by a casual yawn. The reason for them is simple: they're a visceral response to the putrid stench hanging in the air and growing thicker by the minute. Sewage sludge is the closest thing I can compare this foul smell to, but the intensity is on a whole other level—worse than living in a sewer. It's so bad, I fear taking a deep breath will cause the mucky air to melt my internal organs.

Where in the world am I? With the information available to me now, most people would probably conclude I am in a garbage dump or a sewage treatment plant. When I first woke up, the same thought crossed my mind, but…

Pressing my wrist against my nose to block out the smell, I survey my surroundings. The quickest way to describe the scene is as a desert island in the middle of the ocean without anything remotely tropical or pleasant on it. The thing is, not only is the island no bigger than a hundred-square-foot room and deader than a wasteland, but the ocean surrounding it is an eerie, noxious purple. I can hear bubbles rising and popping like some sort of witch's brew roiling in a cauldron.

Where the heck is this place supposed to be?

I don't have the faintest idea where this is. For that matter, I've never seen something in reality that is so obviously a poisonous swamp. It looks just like the miasma marshes in the video games I used to watch my older brother play.

Okay, I'm not getting anywhere trying to figure out where I am, so I'll set that aside for now.

The biggest problem is why the heck I'm in a place like this all alone.

I try recalling what happened before I went to sleep. Familiar images flicker through my mind: I went to my high school in the morning, sat through my classes, and worked just two hours at the café after school. Trying to be considerate of my brother, who's a year older than me and in his senior year of high school, I went straight home after my part-time job. It was an ordinary day from beginning to end.

The only thing different from usual was that I had dived into my bed the moment I'd entered my room. Work had been so chaotic that I was mentally and physically drained beyond exhaustion. My memories cut off there. I probably fell asleep after that. That makes the most sense to me; I'm convinced that's what happened.

But how was I supposed to know I'd wake up surrounded by a gurgling and bubbling poisonous swamp? Am I still dreaming? That question crosses my mind for a whole second, but I can't deny I'm awake when that foul stench is burning all my senses and I have full control of my body.

Luckily, I'm still wearing my outdoor school uniform consisting of a light-brown cardigan over my shirt and a red-and-white pleated skirt. And for whatever reason, I still have my loafers on. This is a popular high school uniform near where I live, but I don't see a single other person around. Maybe it wouldn't have mattered even if I were dressed in my pajamas instead.

SPLAT!

The poisonous muck suddenly splatters onto my small island. A slimy, human-shaped THING crawls onto the island using that muck as a foothold.

"EEP! Wh-What the?!"

"Bwahhh."

The THING rises onto two feet, and the sticky liquid coating its whole body begins dripping off. Something that looks markedly human is left standing there once all the gunk slides off it.

But it's a far cry from an ordinary human. It seems to be wearing

# Another World's Zombie Apocalypse Is Not My Problem!

some rusty armor and has festering sores covering the exposed skin on its face and neck. Plus, its molting skin has faded to a sickly greenish-blue color. Red lines run through its horribly bloodshot eyes, and rotting, gnarly teeth peek out through its wide-open mouth.

The word *zombie* comes instantly to mind. I have only ever seen them in movies, anime, games, and manga, but that *thing's* appearance makes it impossible to think of it as anything else.

"Bwah! Bwoah!"

Staggering, the moaning zombie slowly closes in on my position. I instinctively step back from the grotesque creature. But this is a small island. A few steps and I've reached the end of the line.

A piece of the ledge under my feet breaks off. When that piece hits the poisonous liquid, it disintegrates, leaving behind the sizzling sound of cooking meat.

You've gotta be freakin' kidding me! I'm done for if I fall in!

"Don't you 'Bwah bwah' me! Don't come any closer! Please, just go away!"

"Urg. Aah…aaah…"

"Moan like a baby all you want, zombie, but with looks like that, you aren't winning any cuteness contests. If anything, it only increases your grossness!"

At any rate, what I'm saying isn't getting across to the zombie, as evidenced by the fact that it won't stop coming closer no matter how many times I ask it to go away.

"Th-This can't be real!"

There's almost no space to try to run past the zombie. Even if I did make it by some miracle, this is a tiny island. I can't get away.

As I was trying to think up a plan of action, the zombie had shambled close enough for me to touch if I reached out my hand. It advances on me with its arms lazily hanging in front of it.

"Bwah."

"G-GO AWAAAAAY!"

SLAM!

Desperately wanting to survive, I reflexively shove the zombie's chest with my right hand. Did I use more strength than I thought? The zombie falls onto its back and begins writhing on the ground, moaning.

Am I saved?

I just wish I didn't have to touch a zombie. Partly because you never know what could happen when you touch something unnatural, but mostly because it stinks to high heaven. Case in point, my right hand reeks. This sucks.

"Blehk!" I'm staring at my hand, depressed, when all of a sudden, the zombie's body starts shining brightly. "Whoa?! What in the world?! Why's it glowing?!"

"BWAHHHHHHHHHHHHH!"

The light grows brighter as the zombie screams. It's too blinding to keep my eyes open. However, the light quickly fades. I fearfully open my eyes and blink several times.

The zombie is gone. In its place is a man in his twenties. He's a slender man around six feet tall. His other distinct features are his golden hair tied back in a samurai hairstyle and his pretty sapphire-like eyes.

He's clad in the same type of armor as that zombie, but the luster and polish of his doesn't bear the slightest resemblance to that rust bucket. The armor has transformed from rusty metal into very expensive-looking silver. On closer inspection, he even has a sword hanging from his waist and has the appearance of a noble knight you might find in a storybook.

I'm stunned speechless. Not because I'm captivated by his otherworldly good looks— No, I lied. In all actuality, that has 90 percent to do with it. But there is something else worthier of my attention right now.

I hold my breath.

Um, a zombie just turned into a living, breathing, not-so-dead human.

**Another World's Zombie Apocalypse Is Not My Problem!**

# ◆Chapter 2: Just When I Thought I Figured It Out…

"**BY** the Goddess…have I returned to normal…?"

The now-living knight examines his body as if he can't believe his eyes. I don't know his deal, but I don't blame him for being confused after reverting from zombie to human. That said, I can confidently say I'm even more confused than he is.

I mean, a zombie that was moaning "Bwah bwah" and trying to eat me turned into a human just by me touching it with my right hand. Does this count as bringing someone back from the dead? He *was* a zombie. But considering his filthy armor became clean and shiny, and the way the scream ripped from his throat when he glowed, purification seems like a better explanation. Yep, purification it is.

My eyes meet the knight's while I'm in the middle of escaping reality by analyzing my situation. Having grown up with an older brother, I've never had a problem chatting with boys at school, but while that may be true, I still have reservations about talking to some guy who was a zombie trying to eat me a few moments prior—no matter how cool-looking he is.

"Are you the one who restored me to my former self?"

"I didn't do anything so grandiose. I only touched you with my hand…"

More like I shoved him with all my strength. But telling him that will only draw attention to how violent my method was.

"I knew it… I vaguely remember things from when I was a zombie. I see, I see. That powerful thrust to my chest was your doing," the knight says as he brings his right hand to his chest.

Crud. The fact that I shoved him is completely out in the open!

"I-I didn't hit you because I wanted to. It's your fault for cornering me while groaning 'Bwah bwah'!"

The knight deeply bows his head to me. "Thank you very much."

"Um, er…"

I'm stumped. All I did was touch him—or rather, gave a hard push to his chest— which normally wouldn't do much at all. Even if my joking conclusion that I have the ability to purify zombies is somehow freakishly true, it's not something I've done before. I'm not aware of having an ability like that. Though if purification really exists…I wish it'd purify the horrid odor exuding from my hand!

The knight raises his head and introduces himself. "My name is Lex Irvine, a knight with Grantz Kingdom's Royal Knights."

I could tell he wasn't Japanese by his looks, so I'm not surprised by his foreign name. The issue is with the rest of what he said. I've never heard of Grantz Kingdom.

Between the existence of zombie knights and poisonous swamps, I'm starting to think this is a different world from the one I know. It's a ridiculous theory even to me, but taking all the available information into account, there's a high chance the "another world theory" applies here. Though the biggest mystery is how we're communicating without a language barrier.

"If I may ask, what is your name, fair maiden?"

"Kusunoki— Ah, that's my last name. I'm Mizuha Kusunoki." Since the knight had introduced himself with his first name first, I switched midsentence to match the "local" custom.

"Lady Mizuha… You have a gorgeous name."

This is the first time a man who's not related to me has addressed me by my first name. It's a tad embarrassing, but it's not a bad feeling. But calling me by name isn't the only problem here!

"U-Um, why are you calling me L-Lady? I'm not someone of high status. You can drop that part."

"Because you are the fair lady who saved my life! I must treat you with the respect you are due!" he firmly declares, shooting down my request.

## Another World's Zombie Apocalypse Is Not My Problem!

I was just starting to think he was the gentle-mannered, easy-to-get-along-with type, but it turns out he might actually be the difficult-to-handle type! Even so, he's the only other human around. I have no option but to rely on him right now.

"Excuse me, Sir Lex?"

"Please just call me Lex. I would be most pleased if you spoke with me casually as well."

"I can't do that. I only just met you, Sir Lex."

"LEX! Please call me that."

I knew it. He's the annoying type. Is he just serious to a fault or more stubborn than a mule? Actually, he's probably both. At any rate, it's just a waste of time if I get hung up on responding to his stupid comments in kind.

I take a deep breath and let the tension out of my shoulders. Then I stare at the man in front of me as I tell myself, *All this guy has going for him is his looks. He's a weirdo on the inside. A weirdo. Okay, that should do it!*

"Fine, I'll be casual with you, then. Um...Lex? I have a lot of questions for you. Will you answer them?"

"If it is within my ability to answer you, with pleasure."

"What in the world is going on here? It looks like we're on a desert island in the middle of the deep ocean. We're surrounded on all sides by some sorta venomous-looking muck."

"I don't know what has transpired either. All I can say is that the world suddenly rotted around us, and every person, without exception, turned into a zombie as if in a chain reaction. The only power I know capable of this widespread influence comes from...the Dark Djinn." Lex pauses there and looks at my face. "M'lady, are you feeling unwell?"

"Ahaha. Yes and no. I'm physically fine..." I say, holding my head in my hand.

Zombie-esque things exist. I probably shouldn't be surprised at this point, but not even I could have predicted that a term like "Dark Djinn" would come up so easily as a part of a normal conversation. My zombie apocalypse nightmare has just turned up the fantasy-world ante.

"Uh, stop right there. Every person without exception? I'm not sure I really want to know the answer to this, but is it possible there are no other living humans around?"

"Correct. At least, that was supposed to be the case as far as I know."

"Supposed to be the case?"

"Lady Mizuha...the curse didn't befall you." Lex's expression turns serious as he studies my face. "What in the Goddess's name are you? The Dark Djinn's power is indomitable. None should have been capable of escaping its curse. And yet you—"

"I want to know the answer to that question more than anyone. When I came to, I was here without a clue about anything."

"My inkling might not be so far off after all. That sacred power that allows you to not only break the Dark Djinn's curse but also return me to my former self...I believe it means you are the holy priestess sent here by the Goddess to save our world, Lady Mizuha."

I can't help blinking at that preposterous conclusion. Is this guy all right in the head? Maybe his brains fried when he turned into a zombie.

"Me? A holy priestess? Not a chance. I'm just a high school girl."

"Hi-High? S-Sch...ool? Girl?" Lex tries sounding out the words.

"Oh...my older brother likes to just call me a schoolgirl, but I guess you wouldn't get that either?" I mentioned that with the fleeting hope he might know what that is, but it's no good. Face scrunched up in a confused frown, Lex cocks his head at me. "Well, in any case, I'm just a normal human."

"You can't be. A normal person does not possess the holy powers you used—"

"What I'm trying to say is, don't give me special treatment or look at me funny. I mean, look around. Whatever power I do or don't have, it's not getting us out of here."

The power to purify a zombie and revert them to their original human form. I can't deny that's an awesome power, but it's meaningless if I can't escape this tiny island.

"...Lady Mizuha."

I turn my face aside to avoid Lex's sorrowful gaze. If what he says is true, then there are no other humans aside from us. In other words, we can't expect help to come. Walking through the poisonous swamp to find land is out of the question. To be blunt, there's no hope of being saved.

I never really had any particular ambitions in life, but that doesn't mean I don't enjoy living. As weird as it is for me to say this, I still have a long life ahead of me. I've optimistically lived out my days thinking I

## Another World's Zombie Apocalypse Is Not My Problem!

have plenty of time to find what I want to do with my life... But now I'm going to die in obscurity before I ever discover what that is.

I plop down on the ground with a loud sigh. I pull my knees up to my chin and bury my face in them. Is there a point in living if there's nothing for me to do? There's nothing more painful than endless boredom. Maybe I should just make it easier on myself and dive into that acidic poison...

Negative thoughts overwhelm my mind, my mental state descending into chaos. My one forte is my optimistic energy that gets the regular customers and owners at my part-time job to say, "Seeing you always smile like that cheers me right up too!" but even a cheerful person like me loses hope in a hopeless situation.

The torturous feelings rising inside me turn into tears and spill over. Teardrops drip from my blurry eyes. The drops splatter on the ground.

All of a sudden, the ground faintly glows.

Startled, I spring to my feet.

Wh-What's going on now?!

Once the light spreads over the entire desert island, weeds sprout from the dead earth, covering what had been a wasteland moments prior. As if taking that as the cue, the light scatters as if shattering into pieces, eventually turning phosphorescent and quietly fading away.

"W-Weeds grew...!"

"Indeed...they did grow."

I gape at the ground with Lex. What in the world is happening? Less than a second after my tears hit the earth, the island was covered in green. That's the only thing I know for sure.

"Lady Mizuha...may I ask what it is you did?"

"I-I don't really want to say because it's embarrassing... I just cried a little. When my tears fell, the ground suddenly started glowing."

"To think you returned life to the putrefied ground with your tears... As I thought, you truly are the holy priest—"

"You're just looking for excuses to call me that now."

It seems as if he wants to treat me like some kinda priestess no matter what. I'll admit that bringing plant life back to barren land with just my tears is a holy-sounding power. That being said, I don't want to acknowledge myself as some priestess, regardless of how much power I might have. The reason is simple—everything people view as holy or sacred tends to be beautiful.

Sorry to burst this world's bubble, but I'm no otherworldly beauty. I think I have average looks, but that's about it. It's obvious people will be disappointed when they imagine their priestess as some stunner and then see me. They'll think, *What the heck? That's her?* Then again, this might just be baseless worry when the only people around to disappoint are zombies. Do zombies feel disappointment?

Anyway, Lex is staring at the noxious swamp with hopeful eyes. "While we don't have proof yet, mayhap if you cry over the poison—"

"We might be able to purify it?!"

"Please try it, Lady Mizuha!"

"Okay, leave it to me!" I roll up my sleeves and gallantly stride over to the island's edge. I poke my head slightly over the side and strain my eyes. "Geh! The tears aren't coming! They dried up the second I thought I was saved! Ugggh." At my wits' end, I pound my hands on the ledge. No matter how much I pray for my emotional side from several minutes ago to return, it won't. The pointlessly optimistic side of me has taken full control of my brain.

"Pardon my language, but how about saliva?"

"What are you suggesting with a straight face?"

I knew it, his good looks were too good to be true. There's always a catch.

"Apologies… I simply thought perchance any of your body fluids might work, Lady Mizuha."

"T-True. That is a possibility. But why saliva?"

"Because it seemed the optimum choice. Of course, I am all for trying some *other* options, such as—"

"I'm sorry. I shouldn't have asked. So please don't finish that sentence."

Spitting in public is plenty immodest as it is. I don't want anyone seeing me spit.

"I-I'll try it. Can you face the other way?"

"Why?"

"Obviously because it's embarrassing!"

The day I get labeled as a girl who spits and drools is the day I can no longer get married. Though I guess the chances of me getting married now that I'm in a post-apocalyptic world are close to zilch.

## **Another World's Zombie Apocalypse Is Not My Problem!**

Facing the edge again, I drop to my knees and poke my head over the side. My shoulder-length hair falls into my eyes, annoying me. I brush my hair up and over my ears.

It's not like Lex is watching me, but there's something terribly embarrassing about this that it's making my face heat up. I remind myself I'm doing this to survive and open my mouth to spit the saliva I haven't swallowed yet. Not having had anything to drink for a while has made it sticky. The drop of saliva breaks off from the threadlike trail and finally drips into the poisonous liquid.

There aren't any ripples, but a bigger change occurs instead. The poisonous muck surrounding the island unleashes a blinding light high into the skies. The bubbling and popping stops, and the color turns from a sickly purple to transparent. Last but not least, even the stench assaulting my nose vanishes.

"I-It actually worked..."

"How can this be? As I suspected, Lady Mizuha is the—"

Pushing Lex's new favorite phrase out of my mind, I survey the area around the island. It's blue for as far as the eye can see. It looks just like a beautiful, clean ocean or lake. Not a trace of poison remains.

"Do you think it's really been purified?" I voice my doubts.

"Allow me to confirm." Lex leans over the island's edge and thrusts his hand into the water without hesitation.

"Hey! Are you okay? Your flesh isn't melting off?"

"There is nothing wrong with it. The water is very cool and refreshing," Lex says, dunking his cupped hands into the water and bringing it back to his lips. He takes two loud gulps of it and stares at the water, stunned. "I have never tasted such delicious water before..."

I'm relieved. I don't know what I'd do if something were to happen to him. But once the relief sets in, I become aware of a disturbing fact—my saliva is mixed in with the water Lex just drank. Ew! I start squirming, my face burning hot, when Lex turns to me with a sparkling smile.

"This is the power of your spit, Lady Mizuha!"

"Leave out the part about it being my spit's power! PLEASE!" The heat goes right out of my face, and I dip my hand into the water too. While I'm at it, I scrub the zombie stench off my right hand. The water is cool and refreshing, just as Lex said. Taking a closer look, I realize it's quite clear as well. I can see all the way to the bottom.

"Is it actually really shallow here?"

"It is. This is Lake Nidel. Some sections are deep, but it shouldn't come up higher than your knees in most areas."

"We can walk through it, then."

"We certainly can. Grantz Castle is located in that direction. Let's head there."

I'll turn into a dried-up husk if I stay put on this island, so I decide to go along with Lex's suggestion.

One strange thought occurs to me as we head out: *Was Lex scuttling along the bottom of the lake like some sorta zombie crab?*

**Another World's Zombie Apocalypse Is Not My Problem!**

◆Chapter 3: Apparently, Small Zombies Exist Too

CARRYING my socks and loafers in both hands, I wade through the lake. I could tell just by looking, but the lake is ridiculously large. Pushing forward endlessly hasn't brought the opposite shore into view yet.

Water that comes up to only your knees slows and weighs you down the more you walk in it. I'm athletic, but even my legs are starting to feel like lead. Fortunately, no matter how much I slow down, Lex's back in front of me doesn't move farther away. He seems to be matching his pace to mine. I'm of the opinion he's a nice and serious person, though I have no intention of changing my first impression of him being a weirdo.

After about twenty minutes of walking, we finally arrive at the opposite shore. I flop on the ground like I'm falling over.

"I can't go any farther! My legs feel like logs!"

"Shall we tarry a moment?"

"Please..."

I gaze up at the sky while stretching out my legs. The series of surprises I've experienced since waking up stopped me from thinking about it before, but how do I get back home? To my world? Even an optimist can see that this is a *dangerous* world in every sense of the word. I want to go home right now and live in comfort. The problem is that I don't have the faintest idea of how to make that happen.

I doubt I'll get the answer I want from Lex, but I'll try asking...

"Hey, what would you think if I told you I came from another world?"

"That it only affirms you are our holy priestess."

And that's why I didn't want to ask him!

To my great misfortune, he's entirely useless when it comes to this topic.

"How long will it take to get to the castle from here?"

"We will arrive in no time if we take that path up ahead. It shouldn't take more than half a day."

The path Lex spoke of is located on the raised ground beyond the lake. It's not a walkway paved with concrete or stones, but a dirt trail created by many feet traversing it over time.

Anyway, how in the world is half a day arriving in no time?! I think we have drastically different standards for judging distance, but maybe that's just the way it is in a place where you can't travel by car or train. I'm starting to think I should be glad our journey will end in half a day.

"It figures it'd be rotting here too," I comment, glancing around.

Purifying the lake removed the horrid stench from when I first woke up. But a purplish fog is hovering over the mainland, making the air stagnant and foul. The bark is peeling off from the tree trunks near the path. Naturally, there aren't any leaves on the dead trees, and many of them have snapped in half.

"The Dark Djinn's curse was cast on the entire world. However, we no longer have anything to fear—for we have Lady Mizuha's spit on our side!"

"For crying out loud, stop bringing up my spit!"

If he continues treating me like a real priestess, I fear rumors will spread behind my back that I'm the Holy Priestess of Spit! That's the one thing I never want to happen. EVER!

My feet had dried as we bickered, so I put my socks and shoes back on. I want to rest longer, but I fear relaxing here too long will make me too lazy to walk later. I shove to my feet and dust off my skirt.

"Okay, I've rested enough. Let's keep up the pace until the castle!"

"SO, I've been wondering... Why are we even heading for the castle anyway?" I ask Lex not long after we started walking down the path.

## Another World's Zombie Apocalypse Is Not My Problem!

I didn't question it earlier because I had been desperate to get off that desert island, but now that I've given it some thought, I'm full of doubts.

"Because it is where many people will be gathered, of course."

"What? Didn't you say people aren't around?"

"Yes, I did. You can expect it to be crawling with zombies," Lex answers without hesitation. "It is very likely some are wandering around outside the capital as I was, so there is no guarantee everyone is still inside the city gates as they were before death... But I am positive scores of zombies are within."

"Stop! Stop right there! Is your brain intact?! You must be insane, wanting to go where there are tons of zombies on purpose!"

"I want to purify a great number all at once with your holy powers, Lady Mizuha. Doing so will bring the castle back to its former splendor—"

"Sorry, I'm leaving." I spin around on my heel. I thought I would be safe following Lex, but it looks like it's the complete opposite of that! This is practically walking toward certain death!

"P-Please wait!" Lex runs around in front of me and blocks my path. I understand his desperation to regain his castle as a royal knight, but he's putting the cart ahead of the horse.

"Listen, I'm not against purifying what I can purify. We can't get much accomplished with just the two of us after all. But charging right into the most dangerous place first? Frankly, it's a stupid plan."

"We won't be in danger, for Lady Mizuha is the—"

"Don't finish that sentence if you are going to call me the holy priestess again." My guess is right. Lex falls silent. Exasperation is left in the wake of the anger bubbling up inside me. "I'll admit I might have powers belonging to a priestess, but I'm a normal person on the inside no matter what others want to think. I don't want to strut into a place that's teeming with danger..."

Besides, I've turned only one zombie back into a living person. There's no guarantee the power will work twice. Say it does work—there's a limit to how many zombies I can take on at once. If they surround me, I'm as good as dead. When it comes down to it, I'm just a high school girl. I'm not confident I can see it through to the end.

"Please accept my humble apologies for pushing the plan ahead without trying to understand how you feel, Lady Mizuha... However, with that knowledge, please allow me to ask it of you once more." Lex places his hand over his heart and implores me with dead-serious eyes. "I will protect you no matter what. Won't you please lend me your holy powers, Lady Mizuha?"

"...Lex."

No man has ever sworn to protect me before. My heart skips a beat against my wishes. But my heart-throbbing moment is replaced by sheer shock a second later. A short zombie child lurches out of a tree's shadow beside the path. It teeters slowly toward me moaning "Bwah."

"Geh! Another zombie!"

"Please stand back, m'lady! I shall handle th—" Lex leaps in front of me and locks hands with the zombie, stopping it from coming closer. He moved according to his oath to protect me at all costs.

*He's so brave and sincere!* Seconds after he deeply impresses me, Lex's skin turns bluish purple!

"Bwah!"

"Hey! You just got reinfected!"

I can't believe Lex just turned back into a zombie! This completely ruins how cool he was when he jumped out to protect me! Though this isn't the time to be griping!

I retreat backward at the same time the two zombies shuffle closer to me. Luckily, these zombies are slow. I can probably escape if I run away, but...this is a world full of nothing but zombies, zombies, and more zombies. There's no guarantee I won't run into more zombies wherever I go.

Not much time has passed since I met Lex, but he's someone I've developed a partial connection with in this world. I don't want to abandon him here. I hate to have my right hand smelling worse than manure baking in the sun for days again, but I just have to suck it up.

Zombie Lex's knees suddenly start clattering together, and he breaks into an awkward run. Startled by his unexpected new move, I slap him across the cheek as hard as I can.

"BWAH!" Zombie Lex cries out as he flies backward from my hit and rolls several times on the ground.

Did I use too much strength? While I'm reflecting on my actions, the zombie child charges me. In the time it's taking me to figure out how hard I should touch the zombies, the zombie child is closing the

### **Another World's Zombie Apocalypse Is Not My Problem!**

distance between us.

"Shoo!" I cry out, thrusting my right hand in front of me. Miraculously, that gesture turns into an open-handed slap across the zombie child's face. It falls over backward and writhes around on the ground.

I'm slapping zombies, so it doesn't matter too much, but if I think of them as humans, I'm being pretty cruel. Both zombies start glowing as I'm feeling a little guilty. It looks like the purification power activated without issue.

Obviously, one of the zombies turns back into Lex. His pure-silver armor has regained its glimmering polish. The zombie child transforms into a little girl. A sigh of awe escapes me when I see her. She's prettier than a flower and unlike any other girl I have seen before.

She looks like she's in the last grade of elementary school. Golden hair a brighter shade than Lex's cascades down her long aqua gown detailed with gold embroidery and white lace. Judging by appearances alone, she has that daughter-of-a-rich-family feel to her.

"Y-You saved me, Lady Mizuha." Hand pressed to his head, Lex stumbles to his feet.

"What happened to your promise to protect me no matter what?"

"I have no excuse…"

Regardless of what happened, it's still a fact that he tried to protect me with dauntless courage. I don't blame him as much as I make it sound like I do.

"Good grief," I mutter just as I hear a cute little sigh beside me.

The girl slowly sits up and asks "Wh-Where am I?" as she restlessly looks around.

"What great fortune the Goddess has bestowed upon us…" Lex utters in a trembling voice.

Maybe it's because I saw his pupils dilate, but for a second, I got this image of him as a creeper who preys on little girls, but that doesn't seem to be the case. The girl smiles brighter than the sun as soon as she recognizes Lex.

"Lex…? Are you not Sir Lex?!"

"Yes, it is I, your servant Lex. Thank the heavens you are all right, Your Highness." Lex goes down on one knee and bows his head.

Given that he called her "Your Highness," the girl's status must be higher than just the daughter of a rich family. Whatever the case, I'm the odd woman out here because I don't know anything.

"Hey, Lex? Do you know this girl?"

"I do, m'lady," Lex affirms, turning to face me. He pauses to add an air of importance before introducing her to me. "This young lady is Grantz Kingdom's Princess Cia Greenfield."

The possibility that she was a princess crossed my mind when Lex called her "Your Highness," but it turns out she really is one. I know it's presumptuous of me to say this after finding out, but she definitely gives off that sacred-and-inviolable vibe.

The princess speaks up while I'm too stunned to. "You are the honorable maiden who turned me back, yes?"

"Ah, uh, um... You have the right idea, Princess Highness."

I'm dealing with a princess. Being overly conscious of that fact made me so nervous I word-vomited.

The princess drops her gaze to the ground and lowers her head to me as I'm internally agonizing over my stupid, embarrassing mistake. "How can I ever thank you enough? Truly, thank you. Thank you so very much..."

"D-Don't mention it. I only touched you with my right hand—" I pause as I feel the blood drain from my face.

Lex told me before that he has a vague memory of what happened while he was a zombie. That means there's a painfully high chance the princess remembers my Iron Claw slap to her face. What the heck did I do to royalty?! My left cheek twitches as I stare at my right hand.

"Um, please don't let what happened during the purification process bother you. I am nothing but grateful for what you did! I absolutely won't blame you for it!" the princess frantically declares as she balls her hands into fists.

She's so grown-up for her age. She's just like the pure and virtuous princesses in picture books.

While I'm moved by her maturity, the princess rubs her forehead and nose as she quietly mutters, "Y-You certainly pack quite the punch, though..."

"Ah! I'm sorry! I'm so sorry!"

She does remember! And vividly at that!

"My 'purification' was painfully intense as well... I believe the

## Another World's Zombie Apocalypse Is Not My Problem!

strength you put behind it increased significantly since the first time."

"I'm not apologizing to you, Lex." I glare daggers at him and he guiltily looks away.

The princess glances from me to Lex and says, "You seem like good friends."

"Not in particular," I flatly declare.

"L-Lady Mizuha!" Lex turns a pair of imploring eyes on me.

It's not like I've said anything bad. I mean—

"We only just met several hours ago…"

"You did? I was completely under the impression you had spent far more time together."

It's true that I no longer hold back around Lex. Mostly because he has a few screws loose. He's undeniably a serious and good guy, too, though.

"Lex, can you introduce us?"

"Yes, Your Highness!" Lex introduces me per the princess's orders. "There is nothing to hide here, for the Goddess has sent this fair maiden to save our world as the holy—"

"Okay, stop right there."

"Is something the matter, Lady Mizuha?"

"Yes! Don't give me that look like you've done nothing wrong. You were about to say a word that starts with *pr*, weren't you?"

"Yes, m'lady. Next would be *ie*, then *st*, finally followed by—" Lex says, giving hints in order, to which the princess cheerfully raises her right hand.

"I know the answer! Does that not spell *priestess*?!"

"Correct!"

"Hey! How did this turn into a spelling bee?! And she even got the right answer!"

The princess is all for Lex's games. My head is killing me. I get the feeling I'm going to be introduced as the holy priestess to every person I purify as long as I'm traveling with Lex. Maybe I should just let him stay as a zombie forever? Of course, that's just a joke. It's only a joke…

"Lex likes to call me that, but I'm not someone so important as a priestess."

"I understand, Lady Mizuha. We shall leave it at that."

She seems to have acccpted my opinion because she caught on to how I'm feeling. It makes me wonder if she really understands... You know what, I don't think she does. She's smiling away like she's in on a secret. This has gotta be one of those times when someone thinks they just have to play along! I have to set it straight right now!

I open my mouth to say something, when violent winds carrying a black fog hit me smack in the face. Surprise wins out at first because of how abruptly it happens, but then revulsion almost suffocates me once I realize how bizarre that fog is. The lukewarm wind feels like someone's hands running over my skin. I shudder as all the hair on my body stands up. Disgusting. Creepy.

The wind blows by in a matter of seconds. The thick fog rushes past us at lightning speed. The sickening sensation I felt a second ago is gone.

"Wh-What was that?!" I shout, and I hear a thud right behind me. I look toward the sound and find the princess has fallen on her bottom. "A-Are you all right?!"

"Lady Mizuha... Yes, I am all right. Thank you."

She must've been affected by the black fog. It made me feel nauseated, too, but not bad enough to knock me to the ground. But that's me. Princess Cia is still a child. She may be mature for her age, but it makes sense she couldn't endure the overwhelming fear brought with the wind.

"Please be quiet." Lex touches his index finger to his lips as he grimly locks his eyes on what's ahead of us.

"What's gotten into you all of a sudden?"

"Can't you hear it?"

I incline my head to the side. I don't hear anything that sounds out of the ordinary. Following Lex's lead, I look ahead while straining my ears, and I pick up on a faint noise. It sounds like the commotion out on a school field. The sound grows louder with the passage of time.

"...What is that sound?"

"Ladies, hurry and hide over there!" Lex points to the trees beside the road. Seeing how panicked he is tells me this is no ordinary situation. I step forward to move where he pointed but then stop when I see the princess still sitting on the ground.

"Princess!"

The situation being what it is, I think she'll forgive me being a little rough with her. With that in mind, I tug on the princess's hand and head

## **Another World's Zombie Apocalypse Is Not My Problem!**

for cover behind the trees. Per Lex's advice, I hide with my back pressed against the largest tree in the vicinity. Lex hides elsewhere because the princess and I take up a lot of space together.

Not long after we hide, the noises I'd been hearing sound closer than ever. It's the rumbling, pounding sound of lots of feet chaotically stomping and dragging across the ground to the chorus of "Bwah bwah." That proves it—zombies are here. In droves.

I took shelter without knowing why, but now I want to know what in the zombie apocalypse is going on now. Maybe this is a case of curiosity overcoming fear. I carefully peek around the big tree trunk for a look at the road.

Zombies are walking this way as I suspected. But the number is leaps and bounds beyond what I expected. There aren't just ten or twenty. Fifty? ...No, it looks closer to a hundred. It's the end of the line for us if that horde finds us. I have to touch them to purify them, and I don't have that many hands!

I suddenly feel my right hand shaking. I'm in a hellish situation, so it's not wrong for me to be scared. Or so I tell myself, until I realize the shaking is coming from the princess, not me. She had peeked out at the road as well. The shock had been too much for her; her face is paler than a sheet, and she's shaking harder than the vibrations in the ground.

"Don't worry. I'm here with you." My subconscious awareness of being older has me instinctively embrace the princess from behind with both arms. I drop all formalities and hug her close. I'm worried I've angered her, but that concern seems unnecessary. The princess leans into me as if reassured by my actions.

## Another World's Zombie Apocalypse Is Not My Problem!

I wonder if this is what it would've been like if I had had a sister. Now's not the time for such delusions, but I can't help myself. The princess's petite frame fits perfectly in my arms. She's comforting to hug. Plus, in spite of having been a stinky zombie until not too long ago, she smells sweet like vanilla. Is this princess power?

Thus, the zombie horde begins to pass by us while I'm enjoying my hug with the princess. I was worried sick about what would happen when they got closer, but we can survive without incident if they keep going on their merry way like this. All thanks to Lex for quickly noticing them coming.

Giving him silent thanks, I glance at Lex. Just then, the tree he's hiding behind creaks. It must have been rotten on the inside as well. The tree makes more cracking sounds and snaps in half.

It falls on the ground with a loud KA-BAM! The zombie horde swivels toward him as one and all cry out "BWAH!" as if it's a call to battle. Or maybe a dinner bell in this case?

Lex turns toward me with a tense face. "I-I deeply apologize…!"

"STUPID LEX!"

It's because of Lex that the zombie horde hadn't noticed us up until now. I'm grateful for that—I am—but it doesn't mean much if they find us in the end anyway!

The fallen tree has drawn the zombies' attention to us already. They single-mindedly lurch our way like a bloodhound on the trail. They move at only a brisk walk, but the sheer number of them is what makes it plenty intimidating.

"Run away first, ladies!"

"What about you, Lex?!"

"I will follow right behind you after I slow them down!"

"Sl-Slow them down?! Did you forget you got reinfected doing that earlier?!"

"Please fret not. There are a plethora of ways to get by now that I know not to touch them." Lex draws a real long sword from the sheath at his waist, and something sharp gleams in his eyes.

"H-Hey! D-Don't tell me you're going to cut them with that?!"

Right now, they're deadly zombies, but there's a chance they can return to human if I purify them. We shouldn't kill them if we can avoid it. Lex should know that more than anyone. I sure hope his brains didn't fry some more after being reinfected!

My fears are proved wrong when Lex runs toward not the zombies but the gigantic tree growing beside the road. He drops his knees and swings his sword sideways in a flash of steel. He slices right through the trunk close to the ground, separating the top half from the bottom. Groaning, the giant tree falls across the road.

"Wow…"

I don't care how good you are with the sword—it shouldn't be possible to slice through a tree trunk bigger than the human waist. At least, it's not possible in the world I come from. This is surreal in every sense of the word.

"Lex is the best swordsman in all of Grantz," the princess explains as I stand there dumbfounded.

"He's that amazing of a person…?"

"He does lack in a few areas because he is so serious, which is the one blot on his character."

"That blot on his character utterly offsets the good."

I can't stop from replaying in my mind the scene of Lex courageously taking on the zombie only to be stupidly reinfected. It's going to be pretty difficult to erase this image without something making a bigger impression on me. While it didn't do the trick, his splitting the massive tree in half was pretty awesome.

While the princess and I are chatting, Lex is going around knocking the trees down onto the road. Thanks to his efforts, the zombie horde's forward progress has been drastically slowed, though they haven't completely stopped in their tracks. Some of the horde are walking the long way around the downed trees, while others are sluggishly climbing over them, all the while steadily closing in on us.

"Right, this isn't the time to be casually watching… Can you run, Princess?"

"Y-Yes!" The princess nods, her expression frantic.

I take her hand and break into a run in the opposite direction of the zombies.

HALFWAY through our escape I keep the motion going by kicking

## Another World's Zombie Apocalypse Is Not My Problem!

off the ground every few steps even though we had slowed to a walking speed. I don't know the exact distance we've gone, but I'm positive we've made it a ways. We're currently on top of a small hill. The heavy fog makes it hard to see much, but I can faintly make out an open field ahead of us.

All of a sudden, the right hand I'm holding tugs back. I stop my brisk walk and look over my shoulder to where the princess has sunk to the ground, exhausted. Her shoulders are moving up and down with her heavy breathing.

"A-Are you okay?"

"…I'm sorry. I will stand now."

So she says, but her stamina has reached its limit. Her face is haggard, and I can tell just by looking that she's sweating a lot. Continuing to run in her state could be the real threat to her life. I release her hand and crouch down in front of her.

"Sorry. I made you run at my pace… I think we've put a good distance between us and the horde, so why don't we take a short break?"

"But—"

"Running away now is meaningless if you can't run when you absolutely have to."

"…Very well. Thank you."

"No problem!" I smile at the princess, who sincerely listens to my advice. I love good kids who know when to listen.

I'm cheerfully enjoying the moment until it suddenly dawns on me who it is I'm talking to. Ice-cold sweat trickles down my back.

"I-I-I'm s-s-so s-sincerely s-s-sorry, Princess! I suddenly dropped all formalities with you…"

The desire to protect the princess when I saw her shaking in fear of the zombies took priority over everything else. I think that's what drove out the thought that I need to show her respect. I'm pretty sure that's what did it. It can't be for any other reason.

As I'm desperately trying to make excuses for myself, the princess's eyebrows droop slightly into a sad smile.

"I would be most happy if you continued to treat me as you had before."

"B-But you are a princess…"

"In our situation, the status of princess means close to nothing.

Won't you please do me this favor…?"

It's hard to argue that kingdoms mean anything when the entire world's population has turned into zombies. That said, the power to bring a person back from being a zombie exists in this world. What will happen if all the people revert to normal and the kingdoms are restored? I'm worried the patriotic citizens—or more like the princess's fans—will beat me to death later for my transgressions. Then again, it's pretty pointless to worry about what's going to happen in the future of a world already stuck in a zombie apocalypse.

"…If that's what you want, Princess."

"Thank you…! Also, won't you please call me Cia?"

I no longer have any reason to refuse. However, there is something I want to ask of her as well, so I decide to use this as a bargaining chip.

"Okay, I will if you listen to my request as well. Can you stop calling me Lady Mizuha? It creeps me out and makes me feel weird."

"Then may I address you as my esteemed older sister?"

"What? That's a little much…" My face twitches.

She reminded me of the manga one of my childhood female friends lent me. It was one about an all-girls school where malicious bullying is prevalent and the female main character is saved and encouraged by the "esteemed older sister" she shares her dorm room with. By the end of the story, the two girls are joined together physically and emotionally.

I have nothing against that kind of relationship, but to be blunt, I have zero interest in it. It's not like that's where this is leading, but the mere knowledge of that story makes me reluctant to be called anyone's older sister.

"We aren't really sisters. Okay?"

"I felt greatly comforted when you embraced me behind the tree, Lady Mizuha… It was then that I wondered, if I had had an older sister, would she have been as kind to me as you are."

The princess presses both of her hands to her heart as if storing away a precious feeling. From the look of it, she isn't seeking a *yuri* manga relationship with me.

"Are you…against it?" she appeals, striking the final blow with watery, upturned eyes. It's a killer move coupled with her adorable looks and big green eyes. Since I no longer have a fraction of an objection to the name, I receive a direct hit to the heart. To think my heart would

## Another World's Zombie Apocalypse Is Not My Problem!

skip a beat with a girl!

"I-I guess I can let it pass... Do what you want, Cia."

"...! Thank you so much, Big Sis!" The princess— Cia smiles brighter than the sun.

That doesn't sound half bad. I've always wanted a cute younger sister, so this is turning out to be win-win for us both.

"I feel reenergized after speaking with you, Big Sis. I think I can push myself to go farther now."

"Since we're already here, why don't we rest until Lex shows up? Okay?"

"But—"

"What's this? You won't listen to your big sister?" I say teasingly.

Cia giggles. "All right. Cia will listen to her big sister."

"That's my girl." I pat her on the head with my left hand, which doesn't reek of zombie.

"Ehehe," she happily laughs.

She's cuter than a small forest animal. I made the right choice allowing her to call me her big sister. It's great having a younger sister.

But I'm concerned by how damp Cia's hair feels. She must be sweating more than I initially thought. Several locks of hair are stuck to her forehead. She notices it, too, and brings her left hand up to her forehead to brush back the hair.

"Why does it smell so bad...?" She sniffs her hand with her tiny nose. It suddenly dawns on me—Cia's left hand had been holding my right hand the entire time we ran. In other words—

"Ah, that's the zombie stench—"

"Aaahhh..." Cia unsteadily shakes her head and falls over backward. What just happened? She fainted! Not wanting to leave her like that, I sit on the ground and place her head on my lap.

"LADY MIZUHA! PRINCESS!" a voice shouts from the road we took to get here.

"Lex!"

He's running our way on steady legs while waving his hand. He's not moaning "Bwah bwah," and his skin is the right color. At a glance, he looks safe and healthy.

Lex arrives in front of us and takes a deep breath. His training seems to have paid off because he barely looks tired.

"P-Princess?! What in the Goddess's name happened?!" Lex panics when he sees Cia. I don't want to tell him she fainted because of the stench coming from my hand. Besides, it's not like it's my smell. I'm not in the wrong here. The zombies are at fault.

"Sh-She's so tired from all the running, she seems to have fallen asleep."

"Her Highness does not exercise much… She must have pushed herself too far."

"Yes, that's it. So let's give her time to rest, okay?"

"I can agree to that. Fortunately, I was able to completely throw the zombies off our trail," Lex tells me while looking behind us. Then he lets out a regretful sigh. "In any case, I can't believe they noticed us just as they were about to pass by."

"I was ticked off in the moment, but after thinking about it, I realized it was likely to happen because of how far gone the trees are."

"No, it is wholly my blunder. Knights must always be on full alert for whatever may come their way."

He's strict with himself. I keep thinking Lex would be the perfect superman if not for the few screws he has loose. When I think about how easy it is to speak with him without formality, it makes me glad he's the way he is.

"On the other hand," Lex says, returning his gaze to the open field before us. I follow his gaze to find the fog has lifted somewhat. A massive structure I couldn't see before stands in the distance. "The capital is in view because we hurried here."

**Another World's Zombie Apocalypse Is Not My Problem!**

# ◆Chapter 4: Grantz Kingdom

"SEEING it up close is pretty daunting…"

The capital of Grantz is a fortified city, surrounded entirely by tall stone walls you have to crane your neck to see the top of. This kind of structure exists in the world I come from, too, but I've only ever seen pictures of it. I'm totally overwhelmed by seeing the real thing in person.

"Hey, since this is a fortified city…does that mean you were at war?"

Several moats and canals encircle the city walls. We are currently lying low in one of the dried-out canals, but the mere fact they went to such lengths to prevent invasions gives me the sneaking suspicion they had something they were trying to stop from coming in.

"No. Grantz has never gone to war. These defenses are not for us to partake in war, but to keep others from dragging us into wars. The other two major countries have been fighting for many years now…" Cia sorrowfully relates, squeezing my hand.

Incidentally, the zombie stench has vanished from my right hand. I purified a handy poisonous swamp we had passed along the way and scrubbed my hands in the clean water.

"I'm glad your country isn't at war, Cia. I wouldn't really want to purify a country that's war hungry…"

"Rest assured Grantz is a country that symbolizes peace."

"And it is Grantz's Royal Knights who protect that peace," Lex proudly continues after Cia.

"Hear, hear." I nod along with him. "You really are amazing, Lex."

"Nay. This is what a knight is called to be."

"I respect you. I do. Anyway, I'm heading back to my island. Good luck."

"Thank you, Lady Mizuha. Please be safe— Wait! Why are you leaving?! Please come back here, Lady Mizuha!"

I had made an about-face, but Lex throws out his arms and stands in my way. Sighing, I glance over my shoulder at the stone wall.

"This isn't right. What the heck is with those numbers? There are hundreds more than what was in that horde. And that's just what we can see!"

An absurd number of zombies are loitering in front of the city walls. At a glance, I can tell there are more than a few hundred. If it's like this everywhere around the outer walls, then there are thousands of zombies in the area.

"Don't you think it's smarter to purify the lone zombies first? We'll be surrounded by hundreds of them before I can get much purification done, and we won't have the time to look after the people I succeed in purifying. Not to mention we won't have anywhere to run once we set foot inside the walls."

The more people we bring back from zombieland, the more information we can gather and the higher my chances of finding a way home become. But it's ridiculously stupid to plunge into a place crawling with zombies. We would be literally rushing to our doom.

"I hate to say it, but your plan is insane. Or have you put more thought into it than what you let on, Lex?"

"Going forward, I want to keep the citizens you bring back to life with your holy powers as far from danger as possible. However, there is a limit to what I can do alone."

Why is he okay putting me in danger but not the citizens? I really want to know the answer to that one.

"You plan to purify the Royal Knights and have them assist you," Cia says, filling in the information Lex left out.

He nods and explains from there. "The Royal Knights' primary duty is to defend the castle, including patrolling inside the city walls, which leads me to believe they are very likely still inside."

"I won't argue with you on how reassuring it would be to have lots of strong fighters on our side, but—"

## Another World's Zombie Apocalypse Is Not My Problem!

"Aside from my desire to borrow the help of the Royal Knights," Lex says over my objections, "I also believe the sturdy castle is an optimum temporary shelter."

"Those are great ideas, but it's still too dangerous. What's your plan if there are even more zombies beyond the castle walls?"

"The zombies are slow-footed. They can't catch us if we run."

"Supposing there is somewhere TO run," I say with a sigh.

I feel like I'm doing nothing but raising objections. I try to come up with a counterplan, but I have no better ideas than to search out lone zombies and purify them in small numbers. But it's anyone's guess if increasing our number of allies will actually make liberating the capital of zombies any easier.

As it stands, I'm the only one capable of purifying anything. When I consider the possibility of our new allies reverting to zombies on us, I can't say boosting our numbers is necessarily a good thing. Taking all of that into account, Lex's plan to purify a limited number of people inside the castle and use it as both a shelter and a quarantine zone might be plausible after all.

My biggest concern is Cia and her lack of stamina. From what I can see, the distance between the city walls and the castle spire is long. When it comes down to it, will we be able to safely make it inside the castle? Can Cia run that far?

I look searchingly at Cia, and she welcomes my gaze with determination brimming in her eyes. "I will do everything in my power to make it! If I begin to slow you down…please leave me behind."

"Leave you behind? You'll turn into a zombie!"

"If I do…I hope you will come back and purify me later."

She isn't joking—she's serious. I can't believe I'm being so indecisive when this small child has already found her answer. I feel kind of pathetic even when I set aside the fact that Cia is doing this for her kingdom.

Why am I stuck doing something like this? It's not my problem. Those are my strongest feelings at the moment, but constantly running away isn't going to change anything. I exhale and shift stances.

"Fine. I won't raise further objections."

"…Big Sister!"

I hold up my index finger when Cia breaks into a great big smile.

"But you must promise me one thing. I can't stand the idea of leaving someone behind. I don't care how dangerous and difficult it gets—you must fight to survive until the very end. You hear me?"

"Yes!" Cia exclaims.

I answer her with a nod. I made her promise that, but even if Cia trips and is surrounded by zombies, I'll go to save her without hesitation. The reason why is obvious—I never want to see such an adorable girl become a zombie again.

"You heard me, Lex. I'll be counting on you to be our vanguard."

"...Please leave everything to me. I shall put my life on the line to prot—"

"Please don't. What are we supposed to do once you die or transform again?"

"I-I shall protect you while staying alive!"

"Good boy."

I think there's a problem with him thinking I have to be protected, but I'm in the unfortunate position of being a normal high school girl in a zombie apocalypse. I need to rely on him for what he can handle while I focus on purifying zombies and running away.

"First we have to figure out what to do with the zombies loitering in front of the walls."

"I learned from my earlier experience with the horde that the zombies react to sounds within a certain range and have a habit of heading toward the sound. Our best bet would be to lure the zombies away from the walls by making a loud noise."

"How would you do that, Lex?"

"With this."

Lex walks over to a nearby battered cart lying on its side. He hauls it to the dried-up canal and throws it as if throwing a hammer, all the while crying out "HMPH!" The cart draws an arc through the air, crashing down on the ground a good distance from us and shattering with a loud KER-THWACK.

"Whoa! Hey! Uh?!"

I said I'd go, but this is too soon! I'm not mentally prepared yet. Even as I'm reeling in shock, a horde of zombies is moving toward the sound. As slow as they are, their pace is close to a brisk walk. We don't have to wait long for them to be gone from the front gate. Lex leaps out

### **Another World's Zombie Apocalypse Is Not My Problem!**

of the canal.

"Now! Please follow me!"

STUPID LEX! I curse him in my heart, signaling the start of our plan. I stand holding Cia's hand and break into a run after Lex's armored back.

The zombies are still flocking around the shattered cart pieces, ramming into them while groaning "Bwah bwah." Around ten of the hundred notice our presence, but they're already too far from the gate to reach us in time.

We safely pass through the city gates, and the castle town comes into full view. A wide main street extends from the gates straight to the castle, with wooden buildings packed along either side. Though many of the buildings are in a state of disrepair, the spectacle hasn't lost its splendor.

"Huh? There aren't any zombies?!"

I totally thought the castle and city would be crawling with zombies. It's anticlimactic, but it's better for us if there aren't any.

"Let's charge straight ahead—though that seems impossible now."

Lex had been in the middle of giving directions when that familiar "Bwah" groan sounded from the shadows and zombies began to lurch out of the buildings in droves. Five, ten, twenty… They stagger into the street ceaselessly.

"I KNEW IT! They're here too!" I shout.

"This way, ladies!"

The main street splits into two roads following the city walls. Cia and I run after Lex as he dashes down the right road. On top of it being significantly narrower than the main street, it's also dimly lit because of the shadow cast on it by the tall walls. The fog hanging in the air adds even more to the horror movie feeling.

Just as I'm trying to shake the thought of a monster showing up, a black shadow drops down from above, instantly followed by the sound of bones snapping. Cia and I stop as one and fearfully look at the ground near our feet. My eyes meet those of a zombie crawling on its stomach.

"BWAHHH!"

"NOOOOOOOOO!"

A zombie fell down from the sky! Instead of a monster or a ghost, a zombie fell next to us! As we girls are in the midst of screaming our throats hoarse, Lex quickly grabs hold of a broom resting against one of the buildings and slams the zombie against the city wall with it.

"You saved us, Lex!"

"Th-Thanks."

"I promised to protect you."

What a reassuring line. Coupled with his gallant face, he pulled it off as cool as can be. It's just the image is thoroughly ruined by the backdrop being filled with zombies dropping from the city walls like flies.

"Eek!" I instinctively cry out.

"It appears zombies have piled up on top of the city...walls!" Lex sweeps away one of the zombies falling toward his head. Cries of "Bwah bwah" come from all directions, taking away the ability to relax for even a moment. Zombies block our path forward and backward. Lex is frantically intercepting them with the broom, but the situation is growing rapidly worse.

It's practically a given that the zombies out on the main street will show up if enough time passes. I swivel my head from side to side, scanning the area for anything that can help us escape. It's then that I notice the majority of buildings have flat roofs.

"Hey, why don't we use that to go up on the roof?" I point toward the outdoor stairs leading to the roof of one of the nearby buildings. "The buildings are close enough together that I think we can cross them to get closer to the castle!"

"G-Good idea, Big Sis! Lex!"

"As you command, Your Highness!" Lex powerfully swings the broom around in a giant circle, mowing down the nearby zombies. We dart up the stairs using the opening he created for us. "Use me as a step!"

"Sorry!"

There's no time to hesitate. I step on Lex's knee and then his shoulder to get onto the roof once the stairs end. I spin back around and pull Cia up after me. She's so light. I sure hope Lex doesn't think I'm fat after helping Cia up. Those stupid thoughts cross my mind for all but a second until seeing the zombies closing in on us brings me back to my senses. Rotting hands reach for Lex's ankles.

"LEX!"

## Another World's Zombie Apocalypse Is Not My Problem!

Lex jumps a fraction of a second after my shout. He kicks off the staircase rail, lightly flies through the air, and lands on the rooftop.

"Let us be on our way."

Seeing Lex calmly hurry ahead makes me absently wonder, *What the heck is with this superman?*

"CIA, be careful of the wider gap here."

"O-Okay!"

We close the distance to the castle by traveling over the roofs. Sometimes the gaps between rooftops are wider than others, but they're crossable by jumping. It hasn't proved to be much of an obstacle.

I take a gander below. Hundreds of zombies are pressed up against the walls, chasing after us, but none are trying to climb up. They merely groan and moan as they reach their hands up to get us.

"It doesn't look like the zombies can climb."

"So it appears. Let's draw near the castle while we still can."

We steadily progress onward. Along the way, I look at the zombies falling over themselves as they relentlessly chase us, and I think this must be how a pop idol feels, but then I drop the idea since it's rude to think of fans that way. Besides, the only cheers I'm getting from my zombie fans are to the chorus of "Bwah bwah." Occasionally, they shake things up by throwing in a "GRAGH!" and "Arooh." Also, they stink worse than rotten eggs put inside gym socks. Being chased by that stench is almost as bad as being chased by zombies.

"We are going to descend over there!" Lex instructs.

We have finally made it to the other end of the city. I had hoped the rooftops would continue on to the castle itself, but that would obviously be a hole in their defenses if it did. With Lex's assistance, Cia and I safely jump off the roof and hit the ground running.

Perhaps it's because we lured a lot of zombies out before we climbed on the rooftops that not many zombies are roaming in front of the castle. Even with their smaller numbers, there are still too many to dodge them all, so Lex cuts a path for us by shoving the zombies aside with his broom.

Another moat separates the castle from the city, and a drawbridge connects the two. We cross that bridge and arrive at the castle gate. I thought we were just going to go through the gates, but Lex veers off and takes the stairs to the right.

"Hey! Where are you going?!"

"I am going to drop the portcullis to isolate us from the outside!"

If I remember correctly, a portcullis is the name of a strong iron grating that's supposed to be used at gates to prevent entry from the outside. I turn my eyes toward the top of the gate and see the sharp spikes on the bottom of the grate peeking out.

"H-Hold on! You'll crush the zombies if you drop that now!"

The zombies that followed us are right under where the grate will fall! They are spilling into the castle grounds in a line, so the portcullis will impale at least one no matter the timing we drop it at.

"But we must hurry or we are doomed!"

"You can't kill them!"

They are zombies right now, but I can turn them back into people if I purify them. In other words, killing the zombies is the same as killing people. I don't want to make Lex kill the people he's sworn to protect.

"Is there anything? Anything at all we can use to lure them away with?!"

The zombies are drawing nearer as we're standing around dithering. More zombies begin spilling out of the castle buildings, turning the staircase into our only place of escape.

"Big Sis, how about this?!" Cia holds out a rusted helmet as soon as she retreats to the staircase landing. I look toward her and see a complete set of armor laying on the ground. She must have pulled the helmet from there.

"Nice find, Cia! I can use this!"

I take the helmet faster than I think it through and lean half over the staircase, tossing it as hard as I can outside of the castle gate with a sidearm throw.

"Go away!"

The helmet smacks one zombie in the head and clunks onto the drawbridge. The wooden bridge doesn't make as loud of a sound as metal would have, but it still does the job. The zombies make a beeline for the helmet, leaving the portcullis clear of zombies in no time.

"Lex!"

## Another World's Zombie Apocalypse Is Not My Problem!

The portcullis drops at my signal. The sharp iron spikes lock right into the holes in the ground with an earthshaking rumble. Attracted by that sound, the zombies outside whirl around and charge the gate, but the metal grates do a perfect job of keeping them out.

It looks like we've succeeded in isolating ourselves from the outside. Now we can take a break—except it's never that easy in a zombie apocalypse. The zombies that have been spilling out of the buildings within the castle grounds are clamoring up the staircase toward us. A quick look at them reveals the majority as muscle-bound, armor-clad zombies. These have to be the Royal Knights Lex mentioned.

"Cia, run to the top of the stairs! Shoo, zombies! Shoo!" I let Cia run away first as I pick up the fallen pieces of armor and chuck the cuirass, greaves, and gauntlets at the incoming swarm of zombies. But the zombie knights don't even flinch or stagger. Worse, their cries grow louder and they increase their speed.

*I-I have to flee soon too or—*

"URAAAAAAAAH!" Lex rushes past me. I have no idea where he picked it up, but he's charging into the swarm holding a pavis shield large enough to cover the entire body. In one broad sweep, he drives the swarming zombie knights down the stairs and slams them against the nearest wall.

"Lex!"

"I finished isolating us from the outside! Lady Mizuha, please commence purifying them!"

Over Lex's shoulder I make out his desperate profile. Kicked into motion by that expression, reflex takes over, and I run down the stairs. With my right hand I touch the five zombies he has pinned.

As the purification process begins, the area is filled with a bright light. Their skin transforms from a molten bluish purple to that of a normal human, but I don't have the time to watch over them. At a glance, the surrounding area has a good twenty to thirty zombies gunning for us. Doubtless the rest of the castle is teeming with them.

"We can look after the purified later!"

"Roger that! Cia, don't get separated from me!"

"O-Okay!"

Lex immobilizes the zombies, and I purify them in that order. There are a few cases where I could take a chance and purify some more on my own, but I restrain myself. Lex seems to be fighting while paying close attention to where Cia and I are located, so I don't want to create more work for him by making the wrong move.

"Ugggh… Cia, please don't hate me if my hands reek for life…" I whimper, holding my stinky hand far from my face.

"D-Don't worry, Big Sis! If it's your hands, I will sniff them no matter how bad they stink!"

"Uh, you don't have to sniff them!"

As we're conversing, I glance over my shoulder at the people I have finished purifying. All of them are suspiciously examining their bodies with expressions that scream, "How did I return to normal?!" I'd love to explain it to them, but the situation doesn't allow for it right now.

"Tch!"

"Lex?!"

Lex had been taking on three zombies at once and hadn't noticed the crawler latched on to his ankle. He's visibly transforming into a zombie from his feet up to his head. Several seconds later, his face has turned bluish purple.

"B-Bw—"

"As if I'm going to let you say it!" I leap forward and touch him with my right hand, canceling out his "Bwah" groan. The color returns to his face, and he kicks the zombie off his ankle before slamming the shield hard into the zombies in front of him, sending them flying.

"You saved me again…!"

"All I did was touch you. Don't worry about it. Anyway…there are way more in here than I thought."

Additional zombies are coming into the outer ward from the front courtyard and the inner castle gate ahead. About fifty from what I can see. There seems to be no end to the line following behind them.

"My deepest apologies… I completely misread the situation."

"Well, regretting it now isn't going to save us. Our only option is to do whatever we can to survive."

"Indeed!" Lex responds as he knocks down more zombies with his shield.

"Kyaa!"

I hear Cia scream. I quickly turn around to find her on her butt scooting away from the zombies lunging at her.

## Another World's Zombie Apocalypse Is Not My Problem!

*Where the hell did they come from?!* The answer comes as quick as the question. Zombies are dropping down from the outer and inner castle walls like a hailstorm.

"CIA!" I spring into action as soon as I can, but I don't think I'll make it in time. The zombie's filthy, smelly hand is inches from grabbing Cia!

Out of nowhere, a man decked out in full armor tackles the zombie with a kite shield, knocking it back with great force.

## Another World's Zombie Apocalypse Is Not My Problem!

The suddenness of it all leaves me gaping. The man who saved Cia is a whole size bigger than Lex and is built like an ox, his muscles clearly visible even underneath his armor. He's a sullen middle-aged man with distinctive white hair and beard. He was probably among the people I just purified, but…his presence is a cut above the rest.

Swallowing hard, I ask, "Who are you…?"

"I am the captain of the Grantz Royal Knights, *Oden* Jaxor."

S-Someone with a delicious-sounding name just appeared!

## ◆Chapter 5: The Reigning King of Charges

"**YOUR** Highness, are you unharmed?"

"This is an emergency situation. Don't dawdle taking care of me and confront the zombies!"

"As you command, Princess…" Sir Oden taps his fist against his chest, then turns to the others I had purified. "Men! How long do you plan to sit around?! We have returned to the living! We are free to speak and move of our own volition! That knowledge should be enough to move you to arms! Get to work immobilizing the zombies!" Sir Oden's manifesto booms through the castle grounds, clearing the minds of the newly purified knights.

*You rule, captain of the Royal Knights!* I'm mentally raising my glass to him when I notice some of the knights heading toward the zombies without gear.

"P-Please wait! Be careful not to let the zombies touch you, or you will be reinfected!"

"…You have my gratitude for your warning."

The sharp glint in Sir Oden's eyes makes me flinch. I feel like I'm being censured even though he's thanking me.

"You heard the lass! Don't touch the zombies if you don't want to drool and have foul breath again!" Sir Oden barks out another set of orders.

The knights find substitute shields and push back the zombies in groups. Leave it to royal knights to be skilled at suppressing riots. The zombies in the front courtyard are being taken down before my eyes.

# Another World's Zombie Apocalypse Is Not My Problem!

"Right, this isn't the time to be an onlooker! I have to purify them!" I jump into action and start slapping the pinned-down zombies as if we're playing a game of Duck, Duck, Goose. "Excuse me! Please move! I'm purifying them! Yes, just slide over a little for me!"

Growing used to something is a very scary thing—I no longer have any objections to touching the putrid zombies. My biggest complaint is with that foul odor. They stink worse than an outhouse doubling as a pigpen! I've got the horrible feeling my right hand's stench is worsening by the second, but I just have to grin and bear it for now. Once I'm done with this, I'll scrub and scrub until my body is clean again.

I can finally take a breather now that the zombie moans have been eradicated from the front courtyard. I didn't notice before since I was wholly devoted to touching every zombie in sight, but I purified way more than I thought. Glancing over the surrounding area, I can see easily more than a hundred people. Zombies are all I've seen since waking up in this world, so it's super strange seeing living, breathing people.

It's while I'm basking in the moment that I realize everyone is staring at me. It might've gone to my head if I had stellar looks, but I was never blessed with such a thing. My looks are only good enough to have zombies chasing after me, proved by the fact that they really did chase me.

So, why's everyone staring so hard? I arrive at the answer as soon as I put a little thought into it. Yes, the reason lies with my right hand that's even now putting off a horrid stench that could make grandmas swoon. This stinking thing has the power to purify zombies. Everyone here has witnessed its power for themselves, so it's not unreasonable for them to be curious about it.

Even if they have a good reason for it, though, it's incredibly uncomfortable to be the source of everyone's attention. Cia runs to me while I'm fidgeting by myself. She leaps and hugs me without slowing.

"Big Sister!"

"Cia! Are you okay? Did any zombies touch you?"

"Hehehe. You're silly, Big Sis! I would be a rotting, putrid zombie about now if they had. As you can see, your Cia is a bona fide human!" Cia spreads open her arms and informs me of her safety.

Yep, her cuteness level is as strong as ever. I happily nod along with her when Lex shows up at my side next.

"There is no greater joy for me than to see you are both safe, my ladies."

"Looks like you're in one piece too."

"Yes, thanks to you, m'lady."

He thanks me, but I only went around smacking zombies, which is nothing to boast about. Lex is the one who should be praised for putting his life and body on the line to take down the zombies. I'm about to tell him that when a towering shadow falls over us from the side. Sir Oden is here.

"Good work, Lex."

"Captain Oden! I could have never done it alone," Lex says, directing his gaze to me. "All of this was only possible because of this holy priestess—because of Lady Mizuha's power."

This guy just smoothly introduced me as the priestess. And in a loud voice at that. Thanks to him, everyone in the courtyard overheard.

"Did he just call her the holy priestess?"

"She can't be…"

"Yeah, but she did bring us back…"

Everyone doubted the news at first, but they seemed to have been swayed by Lex's words. Before long they start shouting "Yeah, she must be the great and holy priestess!"

I kept telling and telling him not to treat me like a bloody priestess… I'll say it once more: STUPID LEX!

The courtyard begins buzzing with excitement to the point I'm afraid they'll begin chanting "Priestess, Priestess!"

The celebration is cut short when even more zombies spill out of the inner castle gate.

"Geh! There are still that many left…"

At a glance, there are at least twenty. Not too many compared with the hundred plus I took on in the front courtyard, but…if this is a sign of things to come, there must still be hundreds within the castle buildings. Naturally, that means I have to go around touching lots and lots of zombies. This SUCKS!

As depression looms over me, Sir Oden steps in front of me to block the zombies. "Lady Mizuha, I hope you will lend me your power."

"And I hope you will let me refuse with all my might… But since I won't be able to get any sleep tonight if I don't help, I'll go."

"You have my thanks… Lex, I leave Lady Mizuha to you!"

"Yes, sir!"

At Lex's reply, Sir Oden brandishes the massive shield that's a perfect fit for his large body. Apparently, he plans on charging through the zombies. As I mentally prepare myself to follow in his wake, Cia tugs on the back of my cardigan.

"Big Sis!"

"Don't look so worried. I'll be fine." I pat her on the head, getting a reluctant nod out of her.

"…Please be safe."

"I will. M'kay, I'm heading off, then!" I say as my parting words as I dash after Sir Oden's broad back.

"Follow me! We're going to regain control of the castle right now!"

"I know you said we'll regain the castle right now, but…I can't believe it went that fast." My shoulders shake with heavy breathing as I stand there in disbelief.

In short, we finished securing the castle grounds and interior. It didn't take more than thirty minutes. That's an incredible speed considering how many more zombies I took on compared with what was in the outer ward and how big and complex the castle layout is.

"But what do we do about them?"

I point to the wide stone corridor. Dezombified people are hunched over on both sides of the corridor, their faces twisting with pain. Their aches come not from the purification process but from the wounds Sir Oden inflicted on them. In brief, the scene of the zombies being knocked back one after another by Sir Oden's tanklike charge was brutal. To be blunt, he went too far. The purification went smoothly thanks to Sir Oden, but I'm left with complicated feelings on the matter.

"There are none in the lands who can best Captain Oden at charging."

"I'm surprised you guys even compete in that."

Setting aside Lex's dopey smile and his exposition on the "charging industry," I'm just glad to see no one is seriously injured. They're all just bruised and beaten up. Sir Oden may have been holding back, but only he knows the answer to that.

Speak of the devil: the Reigning King of Charges has just come around the corridor corner. He's wiping the sweat from his brow as if to signal the job is done. The dezombified people are giving him the evil eye, but he returns the favor with a hard face. Everyone looks away from him. How heartless.

"Lady Mizuha, you have my thanks for your cooperation." Sir Oden comes over to me and bows his head. No one as old as he is has ever bowed to me before. It's an odd feeling.

"P-Please raise your head. I haven't done anything much. I only hung behind you slapping people."

"I can go on a rampage suppressing the zombies all I want, but it is a meaningless venture without the ability to purify them. We were only able to gain total control of the castle because of you, Lady Mizuha."

He knew he was going on a rampage… I shut my mouth before I accidentally say something about it. I get the feeling he'll think I'm a pain if I continue being humble here.

"O-Okay, I accept your thanks. You're welcome."

"Thank you. I will rush to your aid should you ever need me."

"Thanks. Please do if the time comes!"

Zombies are still all over the place, making this a bad time for gathering information, but I'll ask him if he knows a way back to my world once things settle down. Sir Oden looks like a man with a lot of experience and knowledge. I'm certain he knows something or can at least point me in the right direction.

"On another note, Lady Mizuha, I have a favor to ask of you." Sir Oden breaches this new subject with a mysteriously serious look.

"What is it?" I ask, tilting my head.

"It has to do with the way you say my name."

"Um, Sir Oden?"

"Would it be possible for you to call me o-DEN? This is the correct way to pronounce it."

I was striving so hard not to pronounce his name the same way as the simmered one-pot dish I eat every winter that's also called *oden*! Now every time I say his name I'm going to think of the food *oden*. I'm starving as it is. What kind of hellish punishment is this?

As I'm thinking about how delicious his name sounds, my stomach

## Another World's Zombie Apocalypse Is Not My Problem!

loudly growls. "Ugh…"

Embarrassing much? It's even worse when there are so many people around to hear it too! My face is hot, and I bet it's turned tomato red. I'm holding my growling stomach with both hands, squirming from the shame, when I hear Sir Oden's loud guffaw.

"HA! HA! HA! We were running around a lot. Hunger is nothing to be ashamed of… Lex."

"Yes, Captain. Worry not, Lady Mizuha. We have plenty of food stores."

"Really? You do?"

It's not my fault I jumped on the mention of food like some kind of glutton. My empty stomach is.

"Grantz Castle stockpiles a large volume of food for emergencies such as this. The food is emergency rations, so I can't guarantee the taste."

"We aren't in a situation to complain about taste."

"In that case, let's head straight to the food stores! Foodstuffs is stored in the basement and ground floor of the tower keep!"

In unbelievably high spirits, I journey with Lex to where food supplies are stored in the basement of the tower keep.

"I-It is all rotten…"

"It figures…"

Wooden boxes are piled up to the ceiling of the candlelit, windowless basement. We pulled a few boxes over and checked their contents, all of which were coated in a sickly purple. The boxes were originally filled with hardtack, but most of it has lost its shape.

I had a hunch this would happen. The decay of the environment outside the city and the damage to the buildings were dead giveaways. Considering how things have been going, there's no way the rations would be conveniently intact. I don't think that would change even if their food were canned or freeze-dried.

"I humbly apologize, Lady Mizuha."

"Meh, that's the way it is here. Anyway, it's not like this is your fault, Lex."

"However, your stomach will continue growling if we don't find some food, m'lady."

"Please, PLEASE, don't make this about me."

I eat a lot for a girl, but not enough to be labeled a glutton. I can endure my hunger during an emergency like this—I can...but my stomach is growling as if to refute that thought and say I can't. I'll do my best in the war against hunger!

Endurance for a time is one thing, but it does us no good if we never have any food later either. As I'm racking my brain for a plan, I spot Lex's thoughtful expression out of the corner of my eye. He's rolling what looks like some sort of rotten legume in his hand.

"What's up, Lex?"

"...Lady Mizuha, I have another request to ask of you." Lex's face suddenly presses in close to mine, causing me to bend my neck away from him.

I have no issues talking with boys, but I have little experience with men. Or to be exact, I have zero experience. I can't help being shaken up by his proximity, and it has nothing to do with liking him or not.

"Huh? Back up and tell me."

This is the first time I have seen him look this serious since we met. I swallow the spit that formed from nervousness. About a second after that, Lex finally makes his request known.

"Please give me your saliva, Lady Mizuha."

"Can I punch you?"

**Another World's Zombie Apocalypse Is Not My Problem!**

## ◆Chapter 6: The Holy Priestess of Spit

"**SHEESH!** You should have said so sooner! I was scared, wondering what you might say when you drew so close with a serious face, and then you go and ask for my saliva. You really aren't in your right mind…!"

"My sincerest apologies… My actions lacked forethought."

I had returned with Lex to the front courtyard, and we're now standing in an open corner. Why are we in a place like this? To test Lex's plan to "bury the seeds and see if they produce food by spitting on them."

"That being said, your saliva is a sacred treasure, Lady Mizuha."

"It's not sacred, nor is it some treasure, so please talk about it normally next time."

Anyone who overhears this is going to think it's some sort of perverted foreplay. In my world at least, this conversation is outlandish enough to make most people recoil, thinking you're a deviant.

"But we don't know for sure if it'll succeed or not."

"True, but think back to the desert island I met you on. Grass and weeds grew luxuriously where it was previously arid, dead land after you purified it. If you take that into account, the chance these seeds will grow is high enough to merit trying it."

"Hmm. Don't get your hopes up."

This world being overrun by zombies makes it a far cry from what I know to be the norm, but I haven't even heard of produce being cultivated by saliva in fictional stories. For that matter, say it does work… Doesn't that mean everyone will be eating food grown with my spit? Oh my gosh! Just imagining that makes me so embarrassed I want to dig a hole and bury myself in it.

"Lady Mizuha, everything is ready for you now. Please commence gracing the land with your holiness," Lex says, patting the soil where he finished planting the seeds.

Don't crops need a ton of prep work like fresh soil, fertilizer, and water to grow? Doubts cross my mind for a whole second before I decide to discard them and stop thinking. The moment we decided to grow crops with spit was the moment we strayed far from agricultural basics.

"Got it. Look the other way, then."

"I would like to see you in the act once. May I?"

"Only if you're okay with me not spitting."

"I apologize for my foolish request! I shall look the other way!"

As I watch Lex quickly turn his back to me, my eyes lock with the other knights curiously looking my way. I flash a killer smile, then narrow my eyes, exuding an intimidating aura. The knights make a unified 180-degree turn.

They might be wondering why I'm making such a big deal over nothing, but what can I do when it's embarrassing? I crouch down to make it easier to spit.

Surrounded by a strange tension in the air, I somehow manage to squeeze together some saliva in my dry mouth, then let it drip down my tongue. The droplet of spit hits the ground without a sound and soaks in. A bright light begins emitting from the courtyard. The arid land is rapidly being covered by lush lawn. Surprised cries of "Ooh!" erupt from the people in the area.

Up to this point has been no different from what happened on the desert island, but there is one drastic change. Green sprouts spring up from where the seeds were planted in the ground. Only a brief time passes between when the seeds sprout and when they grow into saplings and then rapidly grow bigger.

It takes only a second for branches to jut out and for adorable white-and-pink flowers to bloom from them. The flowers burst off the branches like fireworks, allowing green fruit, which quickly turns red, to take their places. This new fruit that's slightly bigger than a fist has to be—

## Another World's Zombie Apocalypse Is Not My Problem!

"A-Apples?"

"Yes, those are apples, Lady Mizuha."

I don't know if they're the same as the ones on Earth, but at least this world has some form of apples.

"However, I am astonished to see that the seeds really grew to the point of bearing fruit."

"I'm the most surprised. How the heck were they even pollinated?"

"Your unworthy servant Lex shall taste it first." Lex plucks one of the many apples off the tree and sinks his teeth into it without a moment's delay. His eyes fly wide open, and he begins trembling. "How can it be this sweet and juicy?!"

"Uh, so what's your final verdict? Is it good?"

"They are the ultimate delicacy!" Lex exclaims, giving me a thumbs-up with a broad smile. From the bottom of my heart, I'm relieved. I was terrified about how bad apples grown from my spit would taste.

"Try one, too, Lady Mizuha."

"Th-Thanks."

Lex picks an apple for me too. I'm a little hesitant to try it since I've never bitten into an apple with the skin still on, but hunger has me sinking my teeth into it before I know it. It crisply crunches under my teeth. One of the sweetest juices I've ever tasted gushes into my mouth.

"Mm!" I instinctively moan.

"How is it? Delicious, isn't it?"

"Yeah! I've never had an apple like this before!"

Starving, I tear another piece out of the fruit without a care about what others think. The apple is extremely sweet, but it has a slight sourness to it that only whets my appetite more.

"You can eat the apples!" Lex announces to the courtyard in a booming voice. "They are a tried-and-true delicacy!"

At Lex's invitation, the people watching from afar partake in sampling the apples. They must've been starving, too, because everyone who grabs an apple smiles broadly.

"I don't believe it... She actually succeeded in making apples grow in less than a minute!"

"But this definitely tastes like an apple. What's more, it's delicious!"

We only have apples, but everyone is celebrating like it's a great big party. It's not as if I went through much trouble to make it happen, but seeing them happy makes me happy.

"But how in the Goddess's name did it grow with such a rich honey flavor?"

"The answer is obvious. It grew from Lady Mizuha's holy saliva!"

"Hey, Lex! You're embarrassing me! Stop saying random things!"

"I knew that was it!"

"Gah! Are you really okay with that answer?!"

Not a single person doubts Lex's response. Worst yet, some people even begin to chant, "Thank the Goddess for the Holy Priestess of Spit!"

"NOOOOOOOO!"

It's happened. I've been dubbed the two names I feared most. This is all stupid Lex's fault! I turn a sharp glare on Lex, but he welcomes it with a sunny expression as if he's attained enlightenment.

"You are not looking at this the right way, Lady Mizuha."

"There's a right way to look at it? Who in their right mind would rejoice over being given a title with the word *spit* in it?"

"Spit certainly does not have a very good image."

"RIGHT?!"

"However, that only applies to commoners. Lady Mizuha, your spit is the holy power capable of saving the world... It wouldn't be an exaggeration to call it holy water at this point. When it comes down to it, there's no problem at all."

"Uh, even if you have no problem with it, I totally do!"

*Dear Mother, your daughter is currently in the predicament of being given a nickname including the word spit in another world. Please save me from this embarrassment*— I'm silently seeking help from my mother, when the sky starts to darken.

"It's getting dark out. Is it almost nighttime?"

"An untold number of zombies still prowl the city, but...it appears we should save our purification patrol for the morrow."

"It would be a real load off my back if we did. To be honest with you, I'm beat."

Everything from my waist down hurts, but my calves are especially tight. I've never walked this much before in my life. My muscles are going to kill me tomorrow.

"You have truly gone above and beyond the call of duty today.

## Another World's Zombie Apocalypse Is Not My Problem!

Please leave securing the premises to us and sleep well tonight, m'lady."

"**IS** it really okay for me to sleep here too? Isn't this one of the royal bedchambers?"

"You are Cia's big sister. You can sleep here! I am actually the one who feels apologetic for not being able to prepare a better room for you..." Cia sadly trails off.

The castle interior is filthier than filthy because of being left in disrepair for however long the people have been zombified for. Cia's bedchamber is usable now only because we cleaned and cleaned the horribly dusty mess we found it in.

More than half the furniture in the room was damaged beyond use, so we had it removed for now. With the rest of the furniture gone, all that remains is the bed and the wooden stool sitting beside it. The sheer size of the room without anything in it makes it bleak and stark.

"It's the situation we're in. Plus, when I think about the alternative—camping outdoors where zombies are prowling—I can put up with practically anything."

"True. It is all thanks to you that I can sleep in this chamber again, Big Sis."

"Meh, all I did was go around touching things," I respond with a wry grin and settle on top of the stool.

Cia's bed is right in front of me. It's fitting that a bed for a princess is king-size. This bed was terribly filthy at first, too, but beating the dust out of the blanket that was the most intact made it decent enough to sleep in. It's not the most hygienic thing, but we have little alternative.

"Anyway, it's a real pain not having a change of clothes. My uniform is going to wrinkle if I sleep in it."

Circumstances being what they are, I don't have a change of clothes. Most of the spare clothing in the castle has been devoured by moths or is too caked with dust to use without thorough washing first. I want to avoid wrinkling and staining my shirt and skirt as much as possible. On the other hand, it's too cold and unsanitary to sleep naked.

"I guess I could just remove my shirt and skirt."

As soon as I strike upon the idea, I strip off my clothes down to my undergarments. My bra and underwear are both pink. If I had known this would happen, I would've gone with a color like dark blue so stains wouldn't show as easily, but I would have done a lot of things differently if I had known about this in advance, so there's no point regretting something I can do nothing about.

"B-Big Sister?!" Cia is shocked by my sudden strip show.

"Sorry, sorry. I thought it's fine since it's just you here."

"I-I guess so. It is just me here... Um! Your skin is very pretty...!"

"You think so?"

"I do! Also, you're so big I'm envious..." Cia is gawking at my chest. I'm not flat-chested, but I'm also not big enough to comment on. I was just above average among my classmates. That doesn't change how big they come across to the young Cia, though.

"You will grow at least this big once you're older, Cia."

"Are you certain about that...?" Cia anxiously looks down at her chest.

It'd actually be more of a problem if she was big at this age. I'd worry about her balance. I'm biased, but Cia is best the way she is right now. I slip on my cardigan while I'm thinking about those things. I feel a draft from above and below, but I just have to put up with it.

"All right, I think we should get some sleep now. You must be tired, too, Cia."

"I am. As ashamed as I am to admit it, I could fall asleep right now..." She bashfully nods before her face suddenly darkens. "But are the others all right?"

"You're a kind girl, Cia. I don't think our friendly neighborhood zombies can get in with the gates down, but...even if they manage to break in, they move slow, and the knights should be able to handle them just fine now that they know not to touch them or be touched by them."

We don't have just superman Lex on our side. Oden, the Reigning King of Charges, is here too. I just know he will send the zombies flying again if they rush into the castle.

"Besides," I continue, trying to alleviate Cia's worries, "I'll purify any zombie that happens to get inside."

"You will, won't you? We will surely be all right with you on our side, Big Sis!"

"Yep, I'll protect you, too, Cia. Come here."

## Another World's Zombie Apocalypse Is Not My Problem!

I move onto the bed and have Cia sit next to me. As I'm stroking her hair, she relaxes and leans against me. This inkling of maternal instinct isn't just my imagination. I'm currently acting as an older sister. Little sister's rule. Good riddance, Big Brother!

I'm amusing myself with such thoughts, when I suddenly hear a freaky cry from somewhere. The wail is a mix of "SKRIEEE" and "BWAHHH." That's definitely not the sound of someone in their right mind.

"What was that? Did you hear it, Cia?"

"I heard a creepy screech…"

I wrap my arms around Cia as she clenches my cardigan. Honestly, I'm terrified to death myself. Never did I think I'd hear an eerie noise like that from anything other than a horror movie.

Another shriek splits the air, ripping a small "Eek" from us both. The horror movie screeches are increasing in frequency.

"Pardon the intrusion, Your Highness, Lady Mizuha!"

The bedchamber door is thrown open with a loud bang. Lex barges into the room. I can tell he's panicked from the sound of his voice and the look on his face, but that's a separate matter from me forgiving his sudden entrance into our room. After all, I am currently dressed in little more than my undergarments and a cardigan. The second Lex notices, his face tenses into an expression that screams, "I'm so dead!"

### Another World's Zombie Apocalypse Is Not My Problem!

"Hey! Why'd you suddenly barge in?!"

"M-My deepest apologies! I shall humbly accept a firm slap to the cheek!"

"Forget getting slapped and turn right around! Leave!"

"Yes, ma'am!"

The door slams shut. I might be overreacting, since it's not like he saw me naked, but...don't underestimate how a virgin feels. My entire body feels red hot. I re-dress as the scorching heat in my face wakes me up.

"Sheesh, Lex can be so dense sometimes. Besides, isn't this your bedchamber, Cia? Isn't it bad for him to barge in even if I'm not half-naked?"

"Ahaha... You could say it's a part of his personality."

"He's got a few screws loose, huh?"

He's not a bad person, but he really does a lot of things that could ruin his good-guy image. That's exactly why he's so easy to interact with, but still.

After I slip on my shoes, I open the door. Lex is standing perfectly straight in the corridor, his expression awkward.

"So? What happened? You seemed to be in a hurry."

"I am! It's an emergency!" Lex practically shouts after he remembers why he rushed here. "Zombies have come over the walls!"

◆Chapter 7: The Zombies Are Serious Now

**AFTER** bolting out of the room, we come to the third floor corridor on the front-castle-gate side of the tower keep. We stop in front of a large oblong window with a beautiful design. When I peer through it at the courtyard below, my eyes are met with a swarm of zombies with red, glowing eyes.

Zombies are climbing over the castle walls and running at full speed straight for the inner gates. They don't have the cleanest running form, but they're moving at a speed unimaginable for the zombies we saw during the daytime. These zombies run even faster than humans. A small cry escapes me as I watch the terrifying scene unfolding below.

"They were so slow and sluggish during the day… How did this happen?" I ask Lex.

"I don't know either, m'lady. All I can say is that the change began the moment the moon smirked."

"The moon smirked?"

"Look over there, Big Sister!" Cia points through the window to a round moon colored a more vivid red than blood. With jagged eyes and a curled mouth, the moon looks like a Halloween jack-o'-lantern.

"…Oh gosh, you're right. It's smirking."

"The zombies' eyes glowed red, and they instantly became smarter and faster when that face appeared on the moon."

"Okay, so how are things below?" I ask, keeping my voice calm. Panic washes over Lex's face.

"The knights on guard became reinfected and overran the outer

### **Another World's Zombie Apocalypse Is Not My Problem!**

ward. Now the zombies are rushing for the inner gates."

"D-Doesn't that mean we're in big trouble…?!"

"The inner gates are thick and sturdy. You have my word that human hands, even if transformed into those of zombies, can do nothing to those gates. Besides, it is our very own captain of the knights who is protecting the gate," Lex declares, full of confidence.

A second later, I hear a number of windows shattering on the lower floors. Not a moment after Cia and I share a worried look, Sir Oden flies around the corner from the direction of the staircase—an army of zombies hot on his trail!

"Zombies have broken into the tower keep!" he shouts while knocking back zombies with his big shield. "Lex! Take Her Highness and Lady Mizuha away from here!"

"**YOUR** word is meaningless, you know that?!"

"I-I cannot apologize enough!"

We race down the corridor, retracing our steps back the way we came. An army of zombies is chasing us. I'd love to purify them, but I'll be trampled under their sheer numbers if I get too close. The zombies are that fast and ferocious right now. All of a sudden, the window ahead to our left shatters. A zombie, covered in glass fragments, launches itself into the corridor in front of us.

"Big Sis!"

The zombie lunges for my shoulder with its big mouth wide open. It's too fast to dodge. The only part of my body I know for sure won't be infected if I touch a zombie is my right hand. What will happen if any other part of me makes contact? Well, at the moment, infection is the least of my worries. I won't be walking out of here intact if I'm chomped on by that giant mouth. I-I'll die!

Just as I resign myself to my fate, Lex's gallant profile enters my view. With his shield, he thrusts away the zombie about to take a chunk out of my shoulder. I seem to be safe for the moment. Not quite sure if I'm still alive, I stand there stunned.

"Th-Thanks," I manage to get out.

"No problem. We must hurry!"

Lex's grim expression reminds me of the zombies in hot pursuit of us. I jump back into running for my life.

"But where the heck can we even run to that's safe?!" I shout to Lex.

I hate to think of what state the first and second floors are in if the third is already swarming with zombies. The rooftop doesn't offer much security when the zombies can climb the walls.

"Do you mind returning to my bedchamber?!" Cia calls out.

"I'm pretty sure we'll be sitting ducks there!"

"A trapdoor installed in my room leads to a hidden tunnel! We might be able to escape from there!"

It's as plain as day that Cia is grasping at straws, but we're in a situation where nowhere is safe. We don't have any better options.

"Okay, let's go there! You heard us, Lex!"

"As you command!"

Lex is holding our rear, fending off the zombies coming from behind. I race through the corridor as the vanguard with Cia between us. We had turned only one corridor down from her chambers, so the way back is an easy route I don't need directions to follow. As soon as I arrive at her room, I throw open the door, let Cia and Lex in, and shut and lock it behind them.

Lex slams his shield against the door, reinforcing it to hold back the incoming swarm. A loud crash shakes the door a fraction of a second later. The zombies are body slamming it. Noisy bangs, slams, and scratches continue without ceasing. Great, the zombies aren't going to give up until they destroy everything in their path to get us. The walls and floor are stone, but the door is made of thick wood—it's not going to last long.

"Find the trapdoor while I can still hold them back!" Lex shouts with a face twisting in pain and exertion.

I nod and run over to where Cia is crouched in a corner of the chamber.

"This part of the floor is supposed to move…"

Underneath the filthy carpet is a section of the stone floor where a square has been cut out. The square stone is very heavy, so I kick it a few times to create enough of a gap to fit my fingers under it. Carefully, I shift the square onto the floor in front of me.

"This! Trapdoor! Woulda been…impossible for you to move alone…

## Another World's Zombie Apocalypse Is Not My Problem!

"Cia!" I pant out as I feel the weight of the square cutting into my fingers. "I never intended to use it! I could never run away alone and leave my people behind! But I must do so now to help you escape, Big Sis!" Cia decided to escape not for herself, but to lead me to safety. She's a really good kid, unlike me. Impressed by Cia's determination, I finish moving the square stone away. Stairs seem to lead deep below the floor, but it's too dark to see much else.

"I am about the only person in the world who knows of this passage. Though that doesn't mean much if the zombies can detect us underground."

"We just have to trust it's safe for now, because the alternative is not!"

"Yes...!"

I let Cia descend the steps first and shout over my shoulder to Lex. "Lex, hurry over here!"

"The door is broken! If I leave my post, the zombies will storm the chamber! Please go on ahead without me!"

"Stop sacrificing yourself all the time!"

"I swore to protect you, Lady Mizuha." He is putting everything he has into keeping the door standing, and yet he flashes a confident smile. Is he doing that to reassure me? "Besides, it's not as if I will die. I will just rot a little."

"Don't act so chivalrous when you're a rust bucket of a knight... Stupid Lex."

I don't want to leave him behind. But everything will be done for if I throw a fit here and end up getting killed by zombies. Seeing as the ones earlier were trying to bite me, there's no guarantee they aren't out to kill me. I understand all of that. I understand it, but—

"Go on now! Hurry! I won't last much longer!"

"...I swear I'll come back to save you!" I tell him, and he answers me with a silent, trusting nod.

Once I make up my mind, I move faster than even I expected. After descending into the hidden passage a few steps, I move the square stone with both palms facing up. It snuggly fits back in place. Without the light from the bedchamber, the secret passage is shrouded in pure darkness.

I'm starting to worry we won't be able to see where we're going, until my eyes adjust to the dark and I'm able to make out the faint outline of our surroundings. Huh...I thought it's impossible for your eyes to adjust if there's no light at all. I glance around and spot a small slit through the stone wall to the outside. Given that there are small openings in key places, it seems to be an intentional part of the design. The faint light streaming in through the cracks must be moonlight.

"Please watch your step since it's dark."

Right after I descend the last step behind Cia, I hear an explosive shattering noise overhead. The unique sound of wood splintering easily leads me to the assumption the chamber door has been breached. Lex!

My chest aches as if someone is squeezing my heart. Cia grabs my hand. Is she afraid? Is she trying to reassure me? Considering how kind Cia is, it's probably the latter.

We still don't have an exact idea about how good zombie senses are. Too afraid to talk or let our footsteps echo on the stones, Cia and I stay perfectly still on the floor without making a sound. The zombies might find us... Such fears whirl through me, but strong determination reigns over every other emotion.

I can't let Lex's fulfilled promise to protect me go to waste. I'll absolutely survive through this and purify Lex and everyone else!

**HOW** much time has passed since we hid under Cia's chambers with bated breath? By the time I've begun to lose all sense of time, a sliver of sunlight filters in through the slits in the wall. Morning has come.

"Nngh..." Cia yawns from where she had slept in my lap and looks up at me while she rubs her drowsy eyes.

"Are you awake now?" I quietly whisper.

"Big Sis...I'm so sorry. I can't believe I fell asleep at a time like this."

"No worries. I took a little nap too."

That's a blatant lie—I didn't sleep a wink. I wasn't trying to stay up; I was simply too afraid of the zombies to fall asleep. Staying awake has brought me a bit of a headache, but it's not bad enough to stop me from moving.

"Anyway, do you mind leading the way out of here? The zombies have quieted down, so I think now's as good a time as ever."

"Okay. I can do it."

## Another World's Zombie Apocalypse Is Not My Problem!

Cia guides me down another set of stairs. The tunnel started from the third floor of the tall castle, giving it a significant ways down to go. We take careful steps to ensure our footsteps don't echo through the halls. Several minutes later, we exit into a stark room around fifty square feet large. About the only things of note in the room are a hatch in the floor and a lever affixed to the wall.

"From here we can take an underground aqueduct to the rear garden, but…"

A mind-boggling stench erupts from the opening when Cia opens the hatch.

"Eugh," I groan, pinching my nose.

Cia's eyes are watering. "I-I forgot all water is putrid…."

Because this is almost completely an airtight, enclosed space, the foul odor is leaps and bounds more horrendous than the stench exuding from the open-air lakes and rivers. I'm not kidding when I say continuing to inhale this malodorous air is going to eat away at my internal organs. We're in serious trouble if I don't do something about it soon.

"Can you move away from the hatch for a minute?" I ask Cia, taking her place beside the hatch to peer below.

The distance to the underground aqueduct is about ten feet farther than I expected. The aqueduct is wide enough for one car to drive through with space on either side. Just like everywhere else, the liquid filling the aqueduct is a poisonous shade of purple.

Frankly, I don't want to open my mouth here, but I suck it up and spit below. That familiar holy light begins to light up the dark space. The bubbles stop popping, and the thick purple liquid turns clear. Last but not least, the foul-smelling odor wreaking havoc on my nose is cleanly washed away.

After I deeply inhale the fresh air, I apologize to Cia. "Sorry you had to see me spit. It's disgusting, but it's our only option at the moment."

"Don't be sorry. Your spit that purifies the zombie blight is one and the same as holy water. There is nothing disgusting about it."

How has the world come to this?! Cia has arrived at the exact same creepy conclusion as Lex! I mean, sure, I'm glad she doesn't view me as disgusting, but calling spit holy water is going a step too far toward crazy. I'm getting more worried by the minute that the people of Grantz had their brains fried by the zombification process! I'm seriously scared for them.

"W-We should head down for now... Er, we're pretty high up, aren't we?"

Depending on the water's depth in the aqueduct, dropping down hard could hurt. I once jumped into a kiddie pool and scraped my butt on the bottom. I'd love to avoid that humiliation and injury this time around.

"We can use this to safely descend below." Cia flips up the lever affixed to the wall beside the hatch, and a chain attached to an anchor appears. When I try pulling on it, the chain jangles its way out of the hole. It winds back down on its own when I let go of the slack.

"Oh! We can scale our way straight down with this."

"It's a meaningless defense if someone comes prepared," Cia notes.

"Well, I can't imagine too many people bringing a ladder to a place like this. Anyway, maybe you should descend first? Oh, but that might not be such a good idea if you fall—"

"B-Big Sis! I am not that big of a klutz!" Cia protests, her face turning red.

"Sorry, sorry," I apologize as I hand her the chain. "If you feel that strongly about it, you can go first."

"Thank you!"

Cia drops the anchor over the side and carefully descends using the chain. I'm holding the chain in place just in case, but I'm on edge because it's swaying erratically.

"Be super careful, Cia!"

"I will! I can do this!"

I wonder if Cia is actually a really stubborn girl. She scales her way down to the anchor and triumphantly smiles up at me.

"What do you think now, Big Sis? Your Cia made it down all by herself!"

"Before you celebrate, look where you're standing—"

"Ah!" Cia misses a step and falls backward into the water. There's a loud splash as water sprays around her.

"Oh dear." I smile sympathetically down at her.

A soaking-wet Cia pushes herself up until she's kneeling in the water. Fortunately, she didn't fall from too high and doesn't seem to be hurt, but...she looks like she could cry at any moment.

## Another World's Zombie Apocalypse Is Not My Problem!

"Uggh."

"HUP." I swing the anchor like a pendulum and land perfectly on the walkway beside the aqueduct. When I release the chain, it winds back up to the hatch with a jingle-jangle sound.

"You can really do anything you set your mind to, Big Sis." Cia is squeezing the water out of her dress over the aqueduct. She's shooting me a loathsome look with pursed lips, but her appearance ruins the scariness she's trying to project.

"No, I can't. Aside from being slightly athletic, I'm normal. Anyway, aren't you cold? Are you okay?"

"Ah, I'm fine. I actually feel refreshed."

"Lucky you! We didn't get to wash off all the sweat from yesterday. Hmm, now I kind of want to go for a swim."

I feel sweaty all over. It'd be weird if I didn't after how much I moved around yesterday, but...this is a grave problem that can do a number on a young lady's mental state.

"But I'll have to save it for later because I don't want my heavy, wet clothing to get in the way."

"When we have the time, you should use the castle's bathhouse instead of the aqueduct."

"What?! The castle has a bath?!"

"It does. Although it isn't very big..."

"I don't care about the size as long as I can bathe! But that's awesome! There's a bath!" I accidentally let out a creepy laugh. How could I not? I love baths! I love them to the point I'd stay in the bath forever if time allowed. On that note, I better keep it a secret that I thought their civilization wasn't advanced enough to have baths. The foul smells definitely have a big part to do with that.

"Um, um...can I join you during your bath?" Cia bashfully inquires.

"It's your castle, Cia. Of course you can."

"Thank you so much, Big Sis!"

Cia must be an incomparable bath lover. She's rejoicing more than I am.

"O-kay! I'm suddenly motivated to do this! I've gotta purify tons of zombies so I can enjoy my bath later!"

I feel like my main motivation has changed, but who cares? I'll still be purifying zombies—it'll just be for me.

"Let's do this!" I pump myself up as I think about my future bath.

# ◆Chapter 8: Humans Are More Worrying Than Zombies

**WE** follow the aqueduct until we reach the wall facing the rear garden. Since she's already soaked, Cia steps down into the waterway and peeks through the iron grate.

"How's it look? Any zombies?"

"No, I don't see any in the rear garden."

"Okay!"

Most of the nearby zombies stormed the castle while pursuing the living last night. Because of that, I had assumed there wouldn't be many left loitering in the gardens, but I didn't expect there to be none. It sounds too good to be true, but maybe luck is finally on our side.

I sit down on my butt on the walkway beside the aqueduct. Before me is a groove carved into the wall opposite the outer wall. The lever mounted there is perpendicular to the outer wall, and when I push it with my foot, part of the wall moves down, creating a crawl space big enough for one person to pass through.

"Heh. So that's how it works."

Cia told me about how it functions in advance, but seeing a trapdoor work in person is oddly thrilling. It seems to be constructed in such a way that only the lower stone is slanted, making it possible to move with as little force as possible.

"Okay, I'll go first." I wait until Cia pulls herself out of the aqueduct to crawl my way out of the castle wall. Outside is shrouded with miasma again due to the zombies retaking the castle.

I have only one thought when I see the sorry state before me: Do I have to spit again?

"Up you go."

Cia is struggling to get through the tight passage, so I take hold of her hand and pull her through.

"Thank you very much, Big Sis."

"Mm-hmm, you're welcome. Now that we're out...the real challenge begins here."

We advance through the garden, stepping as softly as possible. I furtively poke my head around the side of the tower keep and discover five zombies lying in wait. One zombie is pressing his forehead against the castle wall like he's reflecting on his actions, while the others are sluggishly wandering around, groaning "Bwahhh bwahhh."

The invigorated zombies last night had red eyes, but these zombies don't. However, that's not enough evidence to rashly believe these zombies won't be reactivated into a super state when they see us. I pick up a stone off the ground and chuck it at the inner wall.

The stone makes a direct hit with a clunk. Reacting immediately, the zombies totter and fumble their way toward the source of the sound.

"They aren't moving very fast."

"I was concerned how we would get by if they were in the same state as last night, but we can handle them like this."

The zombies seem to think there are people on the other side of the castle wall, since they're banging against it, ramming their head into it, and launching all sorts of body attacks. I wait for a few minutes, but no other zombies show up. Now's as good a time as ever to strike first.

"Cia, once the zombies are purified, warn them not to kick up a fuss," I instruct Cia before kicking off and launching a surprise slap attack on the zombies from behind. I smack each of them on the back of the head.

*How do you like that slap attack?!* I think as I hop back a step and watch as the fallen zombies all begin to glow. The dezombification process ends while I swallow a very unfeminine "Booyah!"

Confused dezombified people replace the zombies. Some are about to speak but close their mouths when they see Cia standing there with her index finger pressed to her lips. From the looks of it, all five are knights. If possible, I want their assistance. Explaining the situation to

## Another World's Zombie Apocalypse Is Not My Problem!

them is critical to earn their help.

I swallow my pride and use charades to convey the situation to them by pretending to be a zombie and then showing the purification process, all through hand and body gestures. I put my thumb and index finger together in a circle to ask if they understand. The knights respond with thumbs-up. My explanation got across to them at the price of my humility, as my bright-red face can attest to.

Pulling myself back together, I peek around the corner wall to grasp what I can of the situation in the front courtyard. Of all the horrible things, I come face-to-face with a zombie! I gulp back the scream threatening to rip from my throat. I'm scared to death, and it reeks! But the bigger problem now is that we've been found.

As I'm hesitating over what move to make, two of the knights yank the zombie back to a spot that isn't visible from the rest of the courtyard. I swiftly slap my hand down on the zombie and touch the arms of both the knights who are already beginning to rot from holding back the zombie while unprotected. The newly dezombified person is bewildered like everyone else, but he keeps his mouth shut when he sees Cia take her "shh" pose.

With that done and over with, I take another gander at the courtyard. Luckily, none of the other zombies have noticed us. But my eyes fly open at how many of them are roaming in circles around the courtyard. Their numbers easily surpass a hundred. I'd taken on a few hundred yesterday, but it's not an easy number to stomach.

In any case, our biggest predicament is how to purify this many zombies without being overwhelmed. We can't just charge in from the front like fools...

"Lady Mizuha," a quiet voice interrupts my internal debate. I glance over my shoulder to where two knights are looking at me with determination brimming in their eyes.

"We will draw the zombies' attention from the opposite end of the courtyard."

"Do you see how many there are? That's a reckless plan—"

"Please do not worry over us. We are Royal Knights."

Just saying they're knights isn't very convincing to me when I don't really know much about this kingdom's knights. Though the cold, hard truth is that I can't think of a more effective strategy than the one they suggested.

While I feel bad to ask this of them, I bow my head and say, "Th-Then please do it. But be as careful as you possibly can."

For whatever reason, not only are the knights gaping at me, but they also have nosebleeds. Is it really okay to entrust any kind of plan to these people? I'm worried for them for all sorts of reasons...

"OOOOOOHHHHHHHHH! LADY MIZUHA!"

"LADY MIZUHA! LADYYY MIZUHAAAAAAA!"

The two knights had circled around to the opposite side of the courtyard and are now successfully luring the zombies toward them by shouting at the top of their lungs. The hundred or so zombies turn their backs on me and hobble toward the knights. I guess you could call this plan a success... But...

"H-Hey! What's the big idea?! Please don't shout my name to lure in zombies!"

"You are such a sinful woman, Big Sis."

"Hoooow?! I don't want to hear that from you too, Cia. What sin have I committed?!"

Even the knights standing defensively behind Cia are nodding. I don't know how or why, but apparently I've committed some great wrong.

"A-Anyway! I'm off to purify the zombies while their attention is being drawn by the others. Watch my back!"

I rush into the fray with the remaining three knights. The zombies don't take notice of my approach. The "Lady Mizuha" call is louder than my stealthy steps. There's nothing more embarrassing than hearing your name being shouted, but I just have to put up with it for now.

I whack each zombie on the back as I run around the courtyard. Occasionally, one reacts to my presence, but I'm able to escape unscathed because of how few actually respond and because of the knights who have my back. I spend the rest of the time rapidly purifying everyone until there's not a zombie left in the front courtyard.

As the dezombified people are adapting to being human again, I rush over to the knights who acted as bait. They're both collapsed on the ground exhausted, their shoulders shaking with heavy breathing.

## Another World's Zombie Apocalypse Is Not My Problem!

"I was able to safely bring everyone back thanks to your courage. Thank you very much."

"We didn't do a whole lot other than retreat while yelling."

"Ah, about that! Why did you shout my name?!"

"Erm...how can we explain? ...Let's just say it's a secret."

"Hah," I sigh. "Well, you pulled it off, so whatever. Just know that you embarrassed me beyond embarrassment!"

I'm grateful they undertook the dangerous role of being bait, but I can't let what they did pass without a word of complaint. However, the knights react in the complete opposite way from what I expected. Their expressions melt into dorky smiles that perfectly match the kind of laughter that goes "Durhurhur." It's rude to say after they just helped me out, but they're kind of creepy. I quickly run away from them and accidentally bump into another knight.

"I-I'm sorry."

"I can't believe I was saved for the second time by you, lass."

That gruff voice! Could it be?! I look up and see just who I expected.

"Sir Oden!"

"Indeed. Your pronunciation has improved." Sir Oden gives a satisfied nod. Apparently it paid off that I had imagined the food when I said it, though it had the adverse effect of making me hungry.

"Big Sis! Zombies are spilling out of the castle!" Cia cries out. I shift my attention that way to see zombies exiting from the inner gate in droves.

"Whoa! I'm getting some serious déjà vu here..."

"Then the result shall be the same as the last time." Sir Oden scoops up a nearby shield and holds it in a way that covers his whole body. "They took me by surprise last night, but I'll never lose to these slowpokes. Rest easy, lass. I swear on my name as the captain of the Royal Knights that I will trample all the zombies in your path."

"Uh, please don't. They'll turn human once I purify them, you know? Please hold back—"

"CHAAAAAAARGE!"

Ah, it's no use. He's not listening.

I sigh and follow behind Sir Oden as he charges through the zombies and into the tower keep.

"IT figures it'd turn out this way…"

Sure enough, the corridors are covered with injured people. At the very least, they have been dezombified, but after seeing how hurt they are, it kind of makes me wonder if purifying them was the right thing to do.

"ANY ZOMBIES LEFT?! I, Oden, shall be your opponent!" Sir Oden, the culprit behind the mass production of injured, bellows as he takes the vanguard.

*Somebody's full of life,* I muse with a dry smile as I jump up to follow him, but instead of launching into a run, I stagger forward. On top of not getting any sleep, I've been running all day. My body has reached its limit.

But I don't have time to rest. Taking into account the high possibility of the zombies becoming super zombies once night hits, we should purify not only the castle but the city as well. As for the castle, only a few sections are left to search for zombies. The third and final floor of the tower keep is almost completely purified, so it's not too far-fetched to say all I have left to do here is clean up the stragglers.

But while that's true, something is bothering me. Despite having purified hundreds of zombies, I've yet to find Lex. Where are you, Lex?!

As I'm walking around the third floor searching for him, I come across a room without a door. The location alone tells me this is Cia's bedchamber. Hesitantly, I peer into the room. My eyes bulge at what I see there.

"Bw…ahh…"

A lone zombie is brandishing a shield as if covering the hidden passageway. Unlike the other zombies who roam the corridors, it stays perfectly in place. I think about how strange that is until I realize that zombie is Lex, and now it oddly makes sense.

"You protected us this whole time."

I highly doubt zombies have intent. But the zombie before me—Lex—alone is different. Is this a miracle? Or is it possible simply because it's Lex? I don't know. Only one thought sticks with me.

"…You're kind of cool." I flick Lex's forehead with my right index finger. The curse on his body begins to lift, and he returns to his human

## Another World's Zombie Apocalypse Is Not My Problem!

form. Eventually, he regains consciousness, and blinks several times, as if he can't wrap his head around the situation.

"Lady Mizuha... What have I—"

"Thank you. Also...welcome back," I say with a smile. I thought these were the things I should tell him before anything else. Lex looks baffled, but he pieces the situation together on his own. A tranquil smile immediately graces his lips.

"I'm back, Lady Mizuha."

How strange. I feel at peace when I'm with Lex. Maybe it's because he's the very first person I met in this world. As those thoughts are going through my mind, my vision suddenly sways. I fall on the ground with a thud. Lex is shouting something, but it sounds so far away.

Weird... What happened to me? It wasn't until I asked myself that question that I realized for the first time that I had fainted.

# ◆Chapter 9: A Reliable Little Scholar

I jerk awake. My vision is blurry from just waking up. My brain isn't working well either. I instinctively think I have to go to school soon or I'll be late. I try to crawl out of bed—one that feels much softer than usual.

"Urk," I cry out when I hit my stomach on something. The impact wakes me right up. I look down and see a girl clad in a dress crying as she hugs me.

"Big Sister!"

"...Cia?"

"Yes, I am your Cia. I am so relieved you came to..."

Instantly, Cia's surreal elegance and loveliness call to mind the extraordinary past few days.

"Ahh, right. I fainted after helping Lex."

"You had been running around the entire time since the prior day... You must have been exhausted."

Physical fatigue was definitely a part of it, but it felt more like I was hit with lethargy from the inside. I think the source was this mysterious power I've never used before—the power to purify. I have to be careful with how I use it from now on, just in case it isn't as limitless as I thought.

"Oh yeah!" I snap back to my senses. "How long was I asleep for? It's not night yet, is it?"

"I-It isn't, but it will be nighttime soon."

I follow Cia's gaze out the bedchamber's window. Outside is slowly

## Another World's Zombie Apocalypse Is Not My Problem!

turning dark; it looks to be around evening time.

"I have to hurry and purify the zombies in the city before nightfall!" I push myself up.

"Big Sis! You can't with your health! Besides, it is already too late for that—"

"But if I don't go now, everyone will revert into zombies... Last night will happen all over again."

We won't ever move forward if we have to repeat our castle siege strategy every time night hits. I would rather take the risk and purify until every zombie is gone from within the city limits.

"As for that problem, we may have an answer," says a knight standing in the doorless doorway. My eyes fly open the second I see that familiar face.

"Lex...!"

"I am glad to see you awake and well."

"Thanks to the hard work of a certain someone."

We smile at each other without saying anything else.

"Okay, care to explain what answer you came up with, then?" I ask, breaking the silence.

"Yes. However, it is not I who will be doing the explaining, but this person here."

Lex steps aside, allowing a short boy into the room. He looks slightly older than Cia. Unlike the knights in their plate armor, he's wearing airy, loose clothing. That, paired with his neatly trimmed auburn hair, gives the impression he's a nobleman's son.

"He is Grantz Kingdom's royal scholar—"

"Pino," the boy cuts Lex off. "Let's not waste my time and get down to business."

He comes off as self-important and cocky. For a moment, I doubt a kid his age could be a scholar, but Cia and Lex acknowledge him as such, so it seems to be true. In any case, I'm not a person of high status who needs to be paid respect, so it doesn't bother me if he wants to act assertive.

"Um, I'm Mizuha. Nice to meet you, Pino." I hold out my right hand to shake hands with him.

"Eek!" he squeaks and hops back. He's clearly avoiding my touch. Did I do something weird? Or does my hand still reek of zombie?

Cia parries my worries with her knowing smile. "Rest assured, Big Sis! I thoroughly cleaned your hands!"

Yep, they aren't putting off a foul odor. What a considerate child she is. Maybe she just couldn't take being around that horrid stench without washing it, but I'm not going to press her on it. Ignorance is bliss.

But if stench isn't the reason, I'm even more at a loss as to why Pino is avoiding me. What if it's a visceral rejection of me? I'll be depressed if it is.

"S-Sorry, but I don't believe in shaking hands. I hope you don't take offense," Pino says, rushing to explain himself.

His panic makes him look his age, instantly erasing the superficially polite impression I had of him. Honestly, I don't get what anyone would have against exchanging handshakes, but I'll go along with it.

"Got it. It's cool if you have a reason."

"Sorry about that. Back to our prior topic of discussion… Getting straight to the point, it is possible to make it through the night. And it's pretty easy to do too." He says it like he's sure of it.

"I have a hard time believing that, after running for my life from the super zombies last night. They ran at ridiculous speeds. I simply can't foresee outrunning them—"

"That's the key right there. Your first big mistake is thinking we have to take them on."

"Are you implying we make it so they can't find us? I hate to poke a hole in your plan, but they targeted people inside the castle they didn't know were there last night…"

"I can see why they would. The castle is full of things zombies react to."

What is he getting at?

My confused head tilt seems to be what Pino expected, because he flashes a satisfied smirk.

"A few zombies were still left here and there in the castle after you fainted. Oh, don't worry. We didn't sustain damage to our numbers, because the knights confined them in the dungeon. But I was able to experiment on those zombies."

"What kind of experiments?"

"Ones that test what it is zombies react to." Pino grins and holds up three fingers as he continues his explanation. "Based on my results,

## Another World's Zombie Apocalypse Is Not My Problem!

I can conclude zombies respond dramatically to three things. First, they react to people who enter their limited range of vision. Second, sound. And lastly, light."

"Light? Like candlelight and fires?"

"Exactly. And what time is light easiest to see?"

"...Right. At night."

That certainly explains why the zombies targeted the castle and broke inside even if they didn't see people. Candles were lit all around the castle last night after all. Torches blazed throughout the courtyards too. I don't think there were many places without light.

I've always had this view that evil things hate light, so the brightly lit castle actually put my mind at rest too. I can't believe that turned out to be the thing that drew the zombies to us.

"Ah! Then the way to get through the night without zombies is—"

"Yes, you're on the right track. We can get through the night by killing all the lights within the castle." Pino smiles victoriously and adds, "See? Easy, isn't it?"

**"MM!"** First thing the next morning, I go out into the courtyard and stretch.

The zombie blighted environment around the rotten capital city has left a dark fog over the sun, but at least the air isn't bad, since I took care of purifying the area within the castle walls. Waking up to such a refreshing morning is only possible thanks to Pino.

Keeping all light off and lying low within the castle saved us from being attacked by zombies last night. Some of them ran around on top of the castle walls, while others rammed the walls, but that seemed to be their normal behavior rather than a reaction to people. It goes without saying that it was a dauntingly surreal scene anyway.

"I see the holy priestess is an early riser." That youthful voice is at odds with its commanding tone.

I turn around to where Pino is walking toward me from the inner gate while yawning. "I had to go around purifying the zombies who came over the walls."

"And secure us food supplies," Pino remarks as he looks around me. Apple trees grew around the courtyard while I was taking care of business. The castle has gone from imposing and stately to a friendly apple plantation.

"Want one?"

"...I actually haven't had a thing to eat since becoming human again. I'll take one."

Pino stretches up to pluck an apple from the closest tree, but he's just a few inches too short to reach it. He must be terribly embarrassed, because he glances at me with a face redder than the apples. He's kind of cute.

Pino jumps out of desperation, snagging one of the apples and ripping it off the branch, dropping leaves on his head in the process. He takes a violent bite out of the apple as if to shake off his humiliation. A split second later, his eyes go rounder than the apple as if he's had a great shock. He's reacting like a character from a cooking manga.

"Th-This is a fairly delectable apple." Pino ravenously devours the crunchy fruit, polishing it off in a matter of moments. He must really like it. "While it's tasty, we'll have a nutritional imbalance from eating just apples, not to mention quickly grow sick of them."

"I totally agree. Not that we have the luxury of complaining."

"We'll have to increase our food options eventually." As Pino goes on about our future, he stares closely at the apple core in his hand. "I've gotta say, though, it leaves a bad aftertaste when I think of this as fruit grown with your spit. Whoa, why do you suddenly look so happy? I'm speaking ill of you. You're creeping me out!"

"Sorry. I'm just so happy to have finally met someone who reacts normally...!"

My sensibilities were starting to tarnish with everyone around me viewing my spit as some kind of gift from God. I'm relieved from the bottom of my heart to finally come across someone with a sane reaction. Pino seems to have picked up on why I reacted that way too. He heaves an exasperated sigh.

"This kingdom is full of easygoing people, after all."

"They're all good people, though."

"I can acknowledge that."

Pino's proud tone lets me know just how much he loves Grantz Kingdom. As a scholar, he can attest to it with his intimate knowledge

## Another World's Zombie Apocalypse Is Not My Problem!

of this kingdom. Speaking of which, I just remembered I had some things I wanted to ask him about.

"Oh yeah, you're a scholar, Pino. Do you know all sorts of things?"

"That's a monstrously vague question. Well, I've been granted the position of scholar at my age. I'm confident in my wealth of knowledge."

"Say, do you know of any items or magic that connects to another world? Hey, wipe that look that practically screams 'What's wrong with this woman?' off your face."

"I merely reacted as you expected I would."

I never thought a boy so much younger than me would turn such scornful eyes my way. It's the kind of look that lays bare just how much of a hopeless case I am, and that kills me on the inside.

"Yeesh, this is what I get for expecting a halfway decent question from you..."

"But you aren't too startled by it, are you?"

"Of course not. You are a strange and unknown being that can purify zombies and nature alike. Nothing startling about bizarre, unfamiliar information coming from you."

"Ooh, you sound kinda smart."

"...Are you making fun of me?"

"Never~~!"

"So you say. I know you're judging me based on appearances too." Pino sulkily turns his face aside. What an understandable concern.

"Well, I'll be honest with you. At first, I was like, 'How's this little kid a scholar?' But Lex and Cia acknowledge you as one, and above all else, I can really tell how smart you are after talking with you like this."

"I guess intelligence just overflows from you when you reach my level, but..."

"Take last night for example. We only got through the night thanks to your brilliant idea, Pino."

"W-We did? Yeah, we did, didn't we? But it only turned out that way with assistance from the Royal Knights. I couldn't have achieved it alone."

Pino is the proud type. Plus, he's sincere when you stroke his ego. I can tell by this conversation that we'll get along great from here.

In a good mood, Pino suddenly becomes talkative. "Now back to your question... When you refer to 'another world,' you mean a different world from the one we are currently standing in, correct?"

"Yep. Huh. Lex knew what I was talking about too. I'm surprised the people here understand the concept of other worlds."

The theory is easy for me to comprehend because we have words and stories about it, but it doesn't come up in everyday conversations. Maybe it'd be easier to understand if my world had a name used across worlds, but I've never heard of such a thing.

"Our god came from another world, so obviously we'd know of it. Why are you bringing this up?" Pino turns suspicious eyes on me, but I couldn't care less about that right now. The important thing here is that he knows of another world.

"Can you tell me more about the world your god comes from?"

"You're frighteningly hung up on this topic."

"That's because it's super important to me."

The world their god comes from and mine might be one and the same.

"I'm more surprised you don't know anything about it. Even small children know about it."

"How could I? I'm not a resident of this world."

"Hold your horses. You just dropped that into the conversation..." Pino buries his head in his hands and crouches on the ground. "Uhh..." he groans.

Thinking he needs sugar to help his brain along, I ask, "Need an apple?"

"I do," he replies. I pick an apple and hand it to him. After he scarfs it down like an animal, he springs to his feet. Holding up the two apple cores as stand-ins for "this world" and "the other world," he begins working out the scenario. "Let me see if I have this right. You unexpectedly came to this world from another one. So you are looking for a way to return to that other—your former—world?"

"Oooh, you're amazing, Pino! You comprehended that much in this little time!"

If I were Pino, this conversation would've ended with me worrying if the other person was in their right mind. It's funny for me to feel this way, but even I think my story is absurd.

"I simply constructed my answer based on what you told me. Anyway, you're making fun of me again."

## Another World's Zombie Apocalypse Is Not My Problem!

"Sorry, I'm just happy you took me seriously, because Lex wrote it off as being obvious since I'm the priestess and didn't give it a second thought."

"Allow me to make it clear that I respect Sir Lex before I say...don't ever lump me into the same category as that meathead."

His face is dead serious. It must mean that much to him. I'll avoid tactlessly aggravating him by dropping the subject here.

"Having said that, I get how Sir Lex feels. After all, while you can believe in the existence of other worlds, it isn't easy to believe someone came from one."

"But you believe me, Pino."

"Don't misunderstand. I am speaking of it as a what-if scenario."

"Tch. That's not fair."

"Now don't get ahead of yourself. This isn't the end of the conversation. I'm of the opinion that nothing will begin if I don't start by believing you, so choosing to not believe you was never on the table for me."

Can I interpret that as him saying he'll try to believe me for now? I don't really get his logic, but I'll be optimistic here and be glad he didn't flat-out reject the idea without listening to me.

"All right, as for our talk about the other world...let's save it for next time."

"What? Why?! Isn't this where we get right into it?!"

"Don't you have things to do right now?" Pino points out, gesturing with his eyes for me to look toward the inner gate. Lex, Sir Oden, and ten or so knights are heading this way.

"Aaah..." I unthinkingly groan aloud. I had completely forgotten about our plans to head into the city to purify zombies.

"Purifying Grantz Kingdom might not seem like your problem, but it's something I need you to do." Pino thrusts up his index finger as he suggests, "How about this? I will answer any and every question you have once you finish successfully purifying all of Grantz's capital."

"That's what it comes down to, huh?"

"It's not a bad plan in my eyes."

Purifying the zombies in the city is a very dangerous job, but at least the danger drops significantly by not moving around at night. All the knights are going to help out too. In all likelihood, I can pull it off without a hitch. Most importantly, I had every intention of purifying the capital anyway, so gaining information about my world in the process will be killing two zombie birds with one stone.

"Okay, I accept your terms."

"A wise decision."

"Oh, but let me correct you on one thing... Purifying this country isn't 'not my problem' anymore. Just so you know."

Pino looks baffled for a moment before his expression gives way to one of amusement. "Not a bad reply for the holy priestess."

"I keep telling you people I'm not your priestess!"

After snorting at my pitiful objection, Pino turns his back toward me and waves. "Happy zombie hunting, 'Miss Holy Priestess of Spit.'"

"GYAH!"

**Another World's Zombie Apocalypse Is Not My Problem!**

◆Chapter 10: The Key to Ridding Exhaustion

**CLANG! CLANG! CLANG!** Zombie moans rise seemingly to the beat of rhythmic metal clashing. Background music that couldn't be called good even to be polite plays throughout Grantz's capital city.

"Here, zombies, zombies, zombies! Come to me!"

Lex is luring the zombies by banging two frying pans together. It's an unbelievably surreal spectacle, but I've grown numb to it after watching it play out since morning. The zombies drawn to the drawbridge leading to the castle gates are felled and pinned to the ground by the knights.

It looks seriously painful every time I see it, but there's nothing for it. Apologizing in my heart, I repeatedly smack zombie after zombie, purifying them in rows. Successfully dezombified people are carried or assisted inside the castle walls.

We've been repeating this process since the early morning, and I have no idea how many people I've purified so far. A conservative estimate would be more than five hundred. And yet, for all that, it hasn't even made a dent in the city's zombies. I'm not exaggerating when I say these numbers can't be taken care of in a day or two.

"Sorry, can we call it a day?"

My consciousness has been going in and out since earlier—I'm at my limit now. Lex looks back at me as he's about to go marching into the city with his frying pans again. My complexion must look like crap, because surprise colors his face.

"I-I sincerely apologize for not noticing. I did not realize you were so worn out..."

"It kinda seems like whenever I purify something, my stamina wears away."

"Mayhap your fainting yesterday was caused by that—"

"Yep, I think it probably was."

Yesterday I not only purified a ton but was also running around like a madwoman, so I might have just fainted out of sheer exhaustion. But this time, dizziness hit me when I've barely moved at all. Purifying is unquestionably the cause.

"Captain Oden, your thoughts?" Lex brings Sir Oden into our conversation.

"We are the ones who will be in a pinch if anything happens to Lady Mizuha. We'll be best served if she takes the rest of the day off," Sir Oden advises.

I feel bad for making them put things on hold on account of me, but forcing myself through it will only lead to me fainting. That will become a true burden on everyone.

"I'm really sorry. You're all doing so much more than I am too."

"I have repeated myself on this subject multiple times, but we only feel gratitude toward you, Lady Mizuha. You're helping us out by resting when you need to," Sir Oden reassures me.

"Thank you."

Going back to my room and getting some sleep sounds good, but I want to wash up first. Fighting to keep from passing out has drenched me in sweat. Aah, if only there were a bath available…

"Big Sister!"

Only one person in the world calls me that. Just as I thought, it's Cia. She's running from the castle as if in a great big hurry.

"What's wrong? Why are you in such a hurry?"

"Nothing is wrong. I just had something I wanted to tell you as soon as possible."

"What is it?" I cock my head.

"Everything is all ready! For the bath!"

The second I hear that word, I frighten even myself by how fast I zoom in close to Cia. "Let's go! Right now!"

## Another World's Zombie Apocalypse Is Not My Problem!

**CIA** shows me the way to the corner room on the northwest end of the tower keep's first floor. Along with Cia, I begin stripping my clothes in what I assume is the changing room. In my world, this is where I'd cover my body with a towel, but no such thing exists here. It's kind of embarrassing, but I enter the bath completely naked.

"Oooh!"

I had assumed the bath would be massive because it's in a castle, but it's smaller than hotel public baths and *onsens*. That being said, it's about the size of five average household bathtubs in a line. Whatever the size, I'm satisfied as long as there is a bath.

"Cia...wasn't it hard getting this ready for use?"

"As for that, the two knights who undertook the dire mission of being bait yesterday offered to help."

"Ah, those two. I feel like I'm always being helped out by them."

"They were more delighted than anything else."

"I'm sure this was one of those scenarios where they fulfilled a lifelong dream by helping out their princess."

"I don't think that was the case this time," Cia says, giggling. I'm curious about what her words imply, but I'd rather submerge in the water than chat. I grab one of the buckets on the ground, scoop up water with it, and swiftly throw it on my body.

"Wooo! This is the stuff! This is nirvana!"

The water is on the lukewarm side but within forgivable bounds. I splash the water onto my body several times. I wrap up the ritual by dumping the last bucketful over the top of my head.

"Phew! I've been brought back to life! Uh, I just thought about it, but isn't water, like, super valuable?! I-Is it okay for me to use this much?"

"We still have plenty of water in the underground aqueduct. Besides, if you grant us use of your holy saliva, we can have as much water as we need..."

"My saliva has no value. I'll give you as much as you need for the sake of baths!"

There's something disturbing about bathing in water cleansed by my spit, but I'm not going to blow this opportunity over it.

"Um! May I ask you to pour water over my head too?!"

"Sure thing." At my beckoning, Cia totters over to me. "Here we go!"

"D-Do it!"

I pour the hot water over Cia's head as she stands there as stiff as a pencil. Her soft golden hair becomes wet and sticks to her dainty body. Her aura of adorableness has been replaced by a sense of beguiling beauty.

It seems she can't bring herself to shake the water out of her hair while standing in front of me. She's staying perfectly still with her eyes pressed shut. It's such a funny pose that it pulls a laugh from me.

"Um, have I done something silly?"

"Nope, you haven't done anything wrong. I was just admiring how cute you are." I collect Cia's long hair behind her back, where I comb my hands through it to squeeze out the water. While I'm at it, I sweep the droplets from her eyelids. "You can open your eyes now. How was it?"

"It felt very nice…!"

"It did? Glad to hear it." I smile in response to Cia's tentative smile.

Talking about stuff like this makes me feel like we're real sisters. In all seriousness, though, there's not even a one in a million chance we look like sisters if you place me next to Cia's overflowing cuteness. Yeah, it's pretty sad when I think about it.

"Okay, next is— Oh, we don't have any soap to cleanse our bodies with. Well, I guess I should just be happy for what we do have under the circumstances."

"Ah, I actually have good news on that front… Do you remember when I was drenched with the water from the aqueduct the other day?"

"I remember it clearly. You're talking about when you fell in the water."

"P-Please forget that part of it! Auuuh," Cia moans, covering her bright-red face with both hands. Is this girl really the same kind of human as me? She's just too cute to be real! Still a little embarrassed, Cia continues speaking. "It's then that I realized the water you have purified has the ability to cleanly wash off filth."

"Oh! Now that you mention it, the water does take the zombie stink right off my hands…"

"It does! So I believe we don't have to worry about the water being unclean!"

"…Boy am I useful, if I do say so myself."

To test out Cia's theory, I scoop up a lock of hair and sniff it—it

## Another World's Zombie Apocalypse Is Not My Problem!

doesn't reek. This is a joyous discovery indeed! I'm actually the type who puts effort into taking care of my hair. I'd given up all hope of maintaining it since coming to this world, but now I might be able to repair the damage. Do your best to survive the odds, my lovely hair!

"Whew, it's getting kinda chilly."

"Let's get in the bath before our bodies get cold."

"Roger that! I'll take you up on that offer!"

I sink into the water up to my shoulders alongside Cia. I figured as much when I was rinsing off, but the temperature isn't hot enough to penetrate my skin, though I can almost feel the heat reaching my center since it's my first bath in ages.

"Phew! I feel regenerated!"

"Me too... It feels really nice."

Never did I think there would be a moment when my heart and mind could be at such peace in a world overrun by zombies. Happiness experienced after overcoming adversity has a completely different taste.

"Thanks, Cia."

"...I am the one who should be thanking you." Cia drops her gaze to the hot water she scooped up in her cupped hands and ruefully expresses her worries. "Now that the world has fallen to this chaotic state...it is my duty as princess to lead the people while Father and Mother are missing. Yet I am incapable of doing anything. I have been made painfully aware of just how much I am relying on those around me."

Water seeps through the cracks in her hands, spilling back into the bath. Mortification and frustration color Cia's face as she gazes at the water slipping between her fingers.

"If you weren't here, Big Sister, the castle would not have the peace it does now."

"I really haven't done all that much. I just happened to have the power to purify and am using it how I please."

"It is not easy to face zombies, regardless of what powers you have."

Cia has no intention of changing her opinion. Though she isn't being stubborn about it either. I think she just has an iron will. That strength is the main reason why she's fretting over how she can be of more use to her people.

"You should be proud of yourself, Cia. You're amazing for thinking about the people around you. Meanwhile, I'm struggling just to take care of myself."

"I am not an amazing person—"

"I'm not going to advise you like I know what I'm talking about when it comes to royalty, but I believe if you want to help your people, the chance will come in due time."

Cia's body is small, appropriate for her young age. Trying to carry the burden of an entire kingdom's future on those small shoulders is no easy feat. Perhaps having to do that despite the difficulty is what it means to be royalty, but in my humble opinion, she doesn't need to push herself to the brink just yet.

"Besides, what do you mean you can't do anything? You're the one who prepared this bath for me. Thanks to restoring my energy here, I'll be able to tackle tomorrow's zombie purification with gumption!"

"...Big Sister."

I scoop up the hot water and toss it at Cia's troubled face. "Take this!"

"Ulp! Wh-What are you—"

"C'mon, you'll really make your people worry if they see their princess with such a grim face." I lunge for Cia and tickle her sides. At first she holds back, but eventually she bursts out laughing. Accelerating my fingers, I pursue Cia as she squirms and tries to get away. "Is this the spot~? Are you ticklish here~?"

"B-Big Sister! N-Not...there!"

I can understand why Cia wants to fulfill her duty as princess. But, as an outsider, I feel more strongly about her being too young to bear all of this. When I was twelve, my thoughts were mostly carefree: *Aw, middle school is right around the corner. Am I gonna have to waste all my time studying?*

While it's not my personal problem, I should wrap up purifying all the capital city's zombies soon for Cia's sake. Finding her mother and father along the way should lift some of the burden off her. Just as I've made up my mind, Cia goes limp in my arms. She seems to have burned off all her energy laughing.

"I-I can't take anymore..."

"...Sorry. I went too far."

**Another World's Zombie Apocalypse Is Not My Problem!**

## ◆Chapter 11: Hi, I'm Boss Lady

**FROM** the morning until the afternoon, I've been doing nothing but touching zombies. At no point in my life did I ever imagine myself spending my days surrounded by a stench fouler than ten rotten eggs stuffed into gym socks and set in the sun to putrefy. The eventual result of pushing through the smelliness for a way home and to help out Cia is—

"That was the last of the zombies in the capital city."

"It's finally OVERRR…!" I fall back on my butt on top of the drawbridge.

No matter how many times I experience the exhaustion that comes from the purification process, I can't get used to it. It's similar to when your arms and legs feel like lead after a hard workout. Purification fatigue is like having exercise exhaustion spread from head to toe. Pressure weighs down on my entire body, making my chest hurt and triggering dizziness attacks. I'm doing okay today, but it's a sensation I'd rather not go through multiple times if I can avoid it.

"You truly worked hard, m'lady. Thank you. Please take the rest of the day off."

"Thanks. You and the knights did good work, Lex… Is no one else resting?"

The knights look ready to go on another zombie hunt. Knights from the outer ward joined the patrol numbers—a total of fifty knights altogether—before crossing the drawbridge.

Sending a sidelong glance to that scene, Lex explains what's going on while holding up his two frying pans. "I said that was the last of the zombies, but only as far as what we could lure here through sound. We can't ignore the possibility of zombies still lurking within buildings, so we are going on a mission to hunt down the stragglers."

The castle is overcrowded with people after all the zombies I've purified thus far. Frankly, it's getting cramped in there. But the problem will be solved if we can guarantee the city's safety. I amble to my feet and pat the dirt off my skirt.

"I'll come too."

"You don't have to. You have already helped us more than enough today—"

"It's all good. I don't mind. I still have strength left because I purified fewer zombies today. Besides, isn't it more convenient to have me around to purify on the spot?" I flash a grin to show him I've still got energy. Wanting to do something about our situation applies to me too. I'm not fond of passing out, but I want to do what I can.

"...Thank you very much, Lady Mizuha. In that case, I shall take you up on your offer."

"Mm-hm. Let's wrap this up!"

I haven't been to the city since we first ran for our lives through it. The sea of zombies prevented me from looking around at the time, but now that I can, I see the buildings are in shambles.

"In this condition, it's going to take a while before people can actually live here even after we liberate it from the zombies."

"That is an inevitable factor we must contend with. We will just have to work together to make repairs," Lex says as he watches our surroundings.

Canals run through the city, and what looks like flowerbeds are located beside many of the homes. I'm sure it was a beautiful cityscape before the apocalypse. If possible, I would love to see it regain its former glory someday.

"But it sure is a relief to have more living people around. The castle has come alive again."

## Another World's Zombie Apocalypse Is Not My Problem!

"That is because zombies were everywhere at first. Now, people being present is much more reassuring than it was before." Despite that being a good thing, Lex doesn't look too happy about it. "However, the presence of people is worrisome in its own right. Various problems arise with an influx of people during a disaster."

"Like spreading the word about not using light and keeping quiet at night," I supply.

"The continued existence of our kingdom hangs in the balance—forcing compliance is inevitable."

"Then there's the food problem."

"People are fighting over apples as it is."

Even if there is an apple shortage, I'd rather not partake in spitting on the ground with the same repetition it takes to pound mochi or knead bread. Well, sure, I'll do it under dire circumstances, but I can't shake the feeling I'm giving up an important part of what it means to be a person.

"I hope to get our hands on grains soon."

"Can we eat bread after that?"

"Wheat and grain need vast plots of lands to grow, so it will have to come after we secure the area outside the city walls."

"Is the bread here crunchy on the outside and soft on the inside?"

"Grantz's bread is the best in the world... It's not an exaggeration to say it's the most supreme bread in the universe. I guarantee the taste and texture will blow the brain juices right out of your head."

"I'll do my best. I'll work for the sake of bread."

Something that blows the brain juices out of your head is a bizarre way to phrase it, but I'll just assume that means it tastes delicious. Part of the reason why I chose to work at my part-time job back home was because of how delicious the owner's homemade bread was. Just remembering it is making me drool, so I quickly clamp my mouth shut. That was close!

But I wonder what kind of bread I can eat here. Immersed in imagining all types of baked goods, a sudden crash startles me. The noise came from inside a two-story house to my right.

"...Is it a zombie?"

"Let's check!"

I follow Lex into the house. As a matter of course, the inside is dusty, the walls have cobwebs, and the wooden floors are cracked and damaged. Tiptoeing so as not to make a sound that'd attract the zombie, we ascend the staircase.

What I see on the second story causes me to blink. It's not a zombie, but a man. He's noisily rummaging through the drawers, squatting on the floor with his butt pointed at us.

"What are you doing there…?"

Jumping at the sound of Lex's voice, the man reluctantly looks over his shoulder. He pulls the kind of face I'd expect to see accompanied by a cry of "Geh!" He looks to be in his early twenties. His wild two-block hairstyle complements his charming facial features, but his looks are ruined by his raggedy clothes.

"We warned everyone not to go into the city because it's dangerous." Lex steps forward intimidatingly. The man scoots back on his butt to reopen the distance.

"Ah, um, well...y-you see! My kid sister has been worried sick about her stuff so much that she can't sleep at night, so I came here to get it for her. This is my house! I ain't doing nothin' suspicious!"

A blatant lie. He's stammering like crazy, and I can see shiny objects that look like they're worth a pretty penny poking out of his pockets and clasped in the hand he's hiding behind his back. Nobody will believe his story.

"I see... Then I'll overlook it this once."

"Holy zombie stench! You believe him?! He's lying through his teeth!"

"H-He is lying?"

Lex seriously didn't pick up on it. There's a limit to how trusting a person can be!

"There's no other way to see it. If he really isn't doing anything wrong, he would have discussed it with you and the other knights first. He's probably stealing that stuff. From the amount he's got on him, I'd say he's stolen from other houses too." I turn a suspicious eye on the man. He scrunches up his face as if he knows the jig is up.

"Tch! And here I had him eatin' the lies outta my hand... You just had to go and say somethin' unnecessary!"

Whoa. He's spewing typical villain lines. I never thought I'd run into someone like this in real life. As I'm enjoying this moment that seems straight out of a story, the man assesses me with his eyes.

"You're the Holy Priestess of Spit, aren't'cha?"

"Not me. You have the wrong person."

"Nah, I know a face when I see—"

"I know no one by that name," I reply emotionlessly. Who in their right mind would acknowledge being called the Holy Priestess of Spit? Even if I go down in history with such a name, I will firmly deny it until the day I die.

"Ruffian! Never use the word *spit* with her name! We will only hear you out after that!"

"I-I don't really get ya, but sure...whatever ya say." The man gives a big nod in response to Lex's frantic persuasion. Good boys. I'm fine as

## Another World's Zombie Apocalypse Is Not My Problem!

long as they get it. "Anyhow, shiny things like these serve no purpose in a world overrun by zombos. Get the picture? Let me off the hook, Miss Priestess. Aren't ya a big shot?"

"I'm no priestess, and I'm not a big shot. For that matter, I don't have the right or power to do anything with you. I'll leave your fate to Lex."

"You heard her. Come back to the castle with me without resisting." Lex shuffles closer to the man.

"Damn it!" the man spits and leaps out the open window beside him.

I quickly run over to look out the window with Lex. The man lands without a scratch and hits the ground running. He's a fast one.

"Lex!"

"Yes, m'lady! I will commence pursuit!" Undaunted, Lex jumps down and gives chase after the man.

I take the less dangerous path by using the stairs before running after them. As you'd expect of two fit adult men, their backs are already a good distance away. The surprising thing is that muscleman Lex is being left in the dust.

"He-he! Nobody is faster than me— Whoaaaaaaaaa?!"

A zombie plops down on the ground in front of the man, coming from the two-story house beside the road. Just as Lex feared, some zombies are still around. The abrupt appearance of the monster makes the man's legs buckle.

"G-Go away! D-Don't come any closer!"

He's chucking his stolen loot at the zombie, but it shows no signs of slowing. "Bwaaah," it cries, drooling as it reaches for him. But that hand never touches the man. Lex repels it with his shield.

"Y-Ya saved me!"

A split second after the man's relieved shout, a zombie appears from the house's first story. Either it's because this zombie isn't going "Bwaah bwaah" or because the man's so utterly relieved that he doesn't realize it's sidling up to him.

"Run away! Zombie to your right!"

My shout finally makes him aware of the zombie. His legs must still be Jell-O because he can't seem to stand up. The zombie wraps its arms around him.

"GAAAAAAAAAH!"

The man's body is rotting before my eyes. I arrive at his side by the time his face is beginning to turn bluish purple. I push the zombie away from him, then follow up with a strong right hand thrust at the man, canceling out his "Bwahhh." My open-handed slap ripped a nonzombie moan from him, but that's just part of the job. At least, that's how I look at it.

"Lady Mizuha, please take care of this one too!"

"Roger that!" By purifying the zombie Lex has pinned, I've secured our safety for the moment. "I can't believe there really are some still left inside."

"Indeed. That was a dangerous spot."

After finishing my conversation with Lex, I hold out my hand to the man who's still sitting on the ground. "Are you okay?"

Just when I think he's too dumbstruck to speak, he mutters, "...Boss Lady Priestess!"

"Huh? Boss Ladyyyy?!"

"The name's Rosso. That was one numbin' hit!"

The man—Rosso—hops to his feet and looks at me with sparkling eyes. The suspicious thug look has been washed clean off his face. It's been replaced with the expression of a boy who's met the girl of his dreams.

"Stop, stop, stop! Why are you suddenly acting like my underling in a gang?! You're clearly older and stronger than me!"

"Age and brawns ain't got a thing to do with it. I was moved by your soul, Boss Lady!"

His 180-degree change confuses me to no end.

"Hey, Lex, talk some sense into him for me!"

"I get it, I totally get it, Sir Rosso!"

"No way..."

Lex places his hands on Rosso's shoulders and nods in strong agreement. "I've been deeply moved by Lady Mizuha's way of life too. I completely, thoroughly understand how you feel...!"

"Lex, my bro!"

"Sir Rosso!"

They firmly cross arms in a brotherly salute. They've totally hit it off together.

Gazing up at the sky, I think, *What the heck is wrong with these people?!*

**Another World's Zombie Apocalypse Is Not My Problem!**

# ◆Chapter 12: Whenever Things Start to Go Well

**EARLIER** this morning, we finally set out to tackle the land beyond the city walls. Overwhelmingly more zombies were roaming outside the city, but I only struggled in the beginning. In open spaces, the zombies were no match for the knights who had learned how the game works inside the city.

Since then, I've been smacking the ever-growing number of immobilized zombies near the city gates. No accidents have occurred so far. While it's been incident-free, there's one big problem.

Said problem is getting in my face during my break inside the walls after smoothly progressing through my workload.

"Boss Lady! Aren't you tired?"

"Ah, nope. I can keep going."

"Boss Lady! Would you like me to massage your shoulders?!"

"Thanks for the offer, but I'm good."

"I'm your underling, Boss Lady! Ask anything of me without holding back!"

"Okay, mind keeping quiet for a while?"

Rosso, the thief I met yesterday, has been hanging around me ever since. Normally, he would be imprisoned for his crimes, but circumstances being what they are, he was let off with a stern warning.

I have no objections to their decision on that front, but I'm starting to wish I had put up more of a fuss if I'd known he was going to be following me around like a dog. Of course, I have no power to overturn this kingdom's rulings anyway.

"Sir Rosso, I feel bad for making you help out when you aren't a knight."

"No worries, man. It's only natural to work together at a time like this."

"You have promise! Let us protect Lady Mizuha together!"

"Aye, Boss Man!"

Lex and Rosso are having a heated conversation. I'm grateful they're thinking of me, but I'd be happier than the zombies let loose on the city at night if they toned it down a little. I'm at a loss for how to deal with them, when Pino, escorted by two knights, comes over to me.

"You've obtained an amusing fellow as a follower in the short time since I last saw you, huh?"

"Hi, Pino... He's less of a follower and more somebody who won't stop tagging along. Ahaha," I say with a dry laugh as I state the truth.

Rosso suddenly starts appraising Pino with his eyes. "Boss Lady... forgive me for the rude question, but who's the little guy? Is he your kid brother?"

"I'm neither a kid nor her younger brother," Pino huffs, facing away from Rosso. He seems really upset about being treated like a child.

"This is Pino. He's supposedly a big-time scholar. You don't know of him, Rosso?"

"Nah. I don't know much about that stuff. I know about Her Highness the Princess, my bro Lex here, and Captain Oden. That's about it," Rosso bluntly admits with disinterest.

"I didn't become a scholar because I wanted fame. I couldn't care less if he knows of me. We have more important matters to tend to... Miss Priestess, I came here because I have a favor to ask of you today."

"Need help with something? I'll give you a hand if it's within my power."

"I want your saliva."

"Hiyaah!"

"Unggh! My nose! My nose is going to fall off!" Pino cries out after I shove my zombie stink hand in his face. He writhes around clawing at his face for a while before springing upright and zeroing in on me. "Wh-What did you do that for?!"

"Hey, that's my line, buddy. Don't come asking for my spit out of

# Another World's Zombie Apocalypse Is Not My Problem!

the blue."

"I simply want to use your saliva in an experiment!"

"Then say so from the start!"

"You're the one who crushed my nose with that fetid hand of yours before I could!"

I don't care how unjust they call me—I'll fight till the bitter end concerning this particular topic.

"Yeesh... For your knowledge, I have zero interest in you. I only see your value as the priestess."

"Wow, that hurts."

"Don't ya worry, Boss Lady! I'm immensely interested in your manliness!"

"O-kay, zip it, Rosso."

"URK!"

I gift Rosso with a face full of zombie stench as well. It lands a critical hit. Rosso has been silenced.

"Hmm, but looking at it another way, when you say you have zero interest in me, that implies there's someone you are interested in."

"...I simply made a verbal blunder. There's no one special—"

"Did you just pause before answering?"

"Argh! Enough! I didn't come here for this drivel! I'm here for the experiment! The EXPERIMENT!"

He's so transparent. I can't help grinning. Pino promised to tell me anything once I've finished purifying Grantz Kingdom. Now I'll just have to ask him who he likes when I ask him about the other world. This is going to be fun...!

"Why do you look so happy?"

"No reason~! Anyway, you brought up doing an experiment, but what do you want from me?"

"Not much. I just want you to purify the moats around the city."

"The place is still teeming with zombies, though..."

"They aren't a problem. Their presence is actually beneficial." Pino flashes an intrepid grin.

What in the zombie apocalypse is he scheming?

For now, I put an end to my break and go ahead with Pino's experiment with the help of the knights. The moat is long, so some zombies are still emersed in the poisonous liquid in the distance. I dribble into the moat while thinking about how I've never purified water when the zombies are in it.

"You can look this way now!" I alert everyone after forcing them to face away from me. Surprised voices rise from them once they turn around. Zombies are painfully writhing in the purified water. Pino tosses a stone, and the closest zombie reacts to it. It slowly stumbles our way.

"They appear more sluggish than usual," Lex observes.

"That one there is floatin' in the water like it's dead."

"Pino, is this what you had in mind?"

Pino seems to have predicted this outcome. He's the only one calmly observing the slower moving zombies.

"My theory was right, then. You see, I got the idea that water purified by you might have some sort of effect on the zombies."

"And this is that effect."

"It isn't powerful enough to bring them back to their human form, but it is capable of drastically weakening them. This is a great discovery." Pino looks as pleased as can be.

Hope blooms on the other knights' faces when they hear of a way to weaken zombies. I, on the other hand, am too troubled by what I see to be genuinely happy. The water around the zombies is darkening by the second.

"Too bad it looks like that effect doesn't last long."

"That sucks. The water's gradually growin' dirtier," Rosso points out.

"If zombies remain in areas that have been purified, their presence brings the blight back. This sequence seems to be the same as it was with the decaying land."

Pino is referencing the time the super-activated night zombies reclaimed the castle, bringing death once more to the greenery and apple trees that had grown in the courtyard after I had purified it.

"Hmm. This is a noteworthy result for the time being. You all have my thanks for your assistance."

"BWEI! BWEI! BWEI!"

A creepy cry cuts Pino's thanks short. I've never heard this sound before. I scan the area for the source until my eyes stop on a dark shadow in the distance. It has a long neck connected to a lengthy torso and four strong legs ending in hooves. From the way its head protrudes from its body, it's definitely not human. It's got to be—

## Another World's Zombie Apocalypse Is Not My Problem!

"A horse...?"

"A zombie horse to be exact."

As Pino has pointed out, the horse is zombified. Its skin is a bluish purple, and a poisonous liquid is foaming from its mouth. I'm more surprised that there's a horse than that it's a zombie horse. After all, I haven't seen a single animal since waking up in this world.

"But it's actin' kinda funny," Rosso notes.

"It's closely watching us." Despite not wanting to look at it, I can't pull my eyes away. It's sickening.

"Why are you here...?" Lex croaks. He's acting like he's just been reunited with a long-lost relative.

"Do you know that horse?"

"That is my cherished mount...Vianta," Lex says sadly, starting to walk toward the zombie horse. But Vianta does the opposite by turning tail and galloping into the wilderness beyond. "Wh-Where are you going? Wait, Vianta!"

Lex's slumps forward, dejected by the horse's departure. He's more depressed than I thought he'd be. It throws me for a real loop because it's so different from how he usually is.

"You'll see Vianta again. She can't have gone too far. We'll find her, okay?"

"As you...say."

"I'll purify her right away the next time we find her. Come on, cheer up."

"...Thank you, Lady Mizuha." Lex exhales a long sigh before raising his head. His smile is clearly faked, but it gets across the point that he's trying to move on. I curl my hands into fists and answer him with an encouraging smile.

Our moment is cut short by a sudden blast of wind. Amid all the surprised shouts, an unsettling feeling stirs in my chest, making me sick to my stomach. I've experienced this eerie sensation before...

Black fog suddenly appears from the direction Vianta disappeared in. It passes over our heads with lightning speed, covering the entire capital.

"This is the same black fog from that time... I've got a real bad feeling about this."

"Do you have some knowledge of this, Miss Priestess?" Pino asks.

"Yeah." I nod once. "We ran into it once on the way to the capital. A zombie horde came right after, as if summoned by it..."

"No zombos coming 'round this time," Rosso reports as he surveys the horizon. He's right; the zombies I can see a ways away from us aren't moving any differently from before.

"You should stop purifying for today," Pino suggests with a hard face. "Even if the zombies aren't reacting yet, they very well could later."

"You mean they'll come at night?"

"It'd be wise to keep the possibility in mind."

It definitely won't be a laughing matter if we fail to prepare and are overwhelmed by a zombie horde at night.

Lex looks torn. "But zombies still abound outside the city walls. Will we truly be capable of protecting the spacious capital city from an attack by the active zombies?"

"Narrow down the space until it's protectable."

"Are you suggesting we evacuate everyone into the castle again? The citizens will feel cramped, but...we have little choice."

"It's better than dying, no?"

At the sound of Pino's decisive tone, the knights in the area brace themselves for what's to come. Is this boy really a child? I'm often left with that question. If nothing else, he's undeniably got a better head on his shoulders than I do.

"I have several strategies in mind. I would like to request the assistance of the Royal Knights... May I, Sir Lex?"

"We are at your command...!" Lex resolutely agrees.

We have no firm proof the zombies are going to attack yet. But an unsettling feeling deep in my chest is telling me they will come.

...I sure hope I'm wrong.

## ◆Chapter 13: Boneless Ham

**THE** evacuation of the people into the castle has been completed, and the knights are preparing to intercept a zombie attack. The black fog is still hanging overhead. Shifting my gaze slightly brings a darkening sky into view. Night is nigh.

"Big Sister…" Cia, escorted by two Royal Knights, comes to my side as I'm absently staring at the sky in front of the inner castle gate.

"What's up? It's dangerous for you to be outside."

"But when I think of what happened last time…" Her thin voice trails off, her lower lip trembling.

I don't blame her for being uneasy. Cia has seen firsthand the zombie horde lured by the black fog and the freakishly stronger night zombies. Smiling, I stroke her hair, brushing my finger along her chilled cheek.

"You're the princess, right, Cia? Everyone will worry if they see you looking like that."

"That is…a good point. A princess shouldn't let her fears show on her face."

"This time is different. We have lots of knights on our side. I'm sure it will work out."

I was concerned those words wouldn't be enough to ease her misgivings, but a commanding aura transforms her worried face to that of a princess. I'm always impressed by how mature she is at times like this.

"Please be careful, Big Sis."

"Thanks. I'll kick some zombie butt for you and the others." I pose with both fists held up and turn to the Royal Knights behind me. "Take care of Cia." They nod reassuringly and return inside the castle with the princess. Lex takes up position at my side as I watch her go.

"You are a truly brave young woman, Lady Mizuha."

"Honestly, I want to run away at lightning speed… Not that there's anywhere I can run to."

"We, the proud knights of Grantz, shall protect you at all costs." Lex raps his fist against his chest.

"I'm counting on you like my life depends on it…because it does."

While I can handle the sluggish daytime zombies, the fact of the matter is that I can't do a thing about the super night zombies alone. As pathetic as it is, I have little option but to rely on the knights.

"Well, let's just hope that nothing happens."

"Even if it does, we are fully prepared for it, m'lady. I don't want to sound as if I am letting down my guard…but it will assuredly be all right."

We have prepared two primary defense measures. One is the ropes we have pulled taut between the grooves in the merlon and the apple trees, creating a web of crisscrossing snares and nets. It's constructed in such a way that zombies jumping from the outer walls into the wards will get caught in it. According to Pino, "with their rot-addled brains, they aren't likely capable of the complicated thought necessary to navigate through the ropes without getting themselves snared like rabbits."

I've played around in a rope jungle-gym used in an obstacle course before, and I clearly remember not making any forward progress when I relentlessly struggled to get out of it. This should work as long as they don't chew their way through the ropes…

The buckets placed beside every knight are the second defense measure. Many more are stationed alongside the walls. Inside is water purified by my spit. Pino's afternoon experiment taught us that the zombies are weakened by purified water. So this defense is putting that knowledge into practice.

Our preparations are as good as they're going to get in the time we have. I don't want a horde to show up, but if they do, we're ready for them. Harboring mixed feelings of apprehension and boldness, I look at the black fog above. Instantly, the visible darkness deepens. Evidence that true night is upon us.

## Another World's Zombie Apocalypse Is Not My Problem!

It's quiet. Everyone is watching and waiting with bated breath. Nothing has happened yet. Had this been a groundless fear all along? I'm okay if that's the case, but...

All of a sudden, the black fog slams down on us. The courtyard is caught in a whirlpool of confusion, but then a strong wind whooshes through, scattering the fog. What the heck was that? I sweep my eyes over the area, but the fog is gone. Maybe the danger has lifted?

I got my hopes up too soon.

Bone-chilling screeches can be heard in the distance, accompanied by the sound of shaking ground from all four directions. Before we knew it, countless silhouettes had appeared on top of the castle walls.

"LIGHT the torches! They're here!" Sir Oden's orders thunder through the courtyard. We'd decided in advance to secure visibility by lighting the torches should they attack even when there was no light.

Flames burst to life all around, instantly brightening the darkness that shadowed our view. No sooner are the torches lit than we see a swarm of zombies on top of the ramparts. Even though an unimaginable number are already running along the walls, more and more keep joining their ranks by climbing up.

Zombies begin jumping off the walls into the castle grounds. The enemy is coming from all sides. We will be squashed under their sheer numbers if they come right at us, but...that's not what happens. They get caught in our crisscrossed ropes, the myriad of snares hooking zombies as they find feet and hands entangled, all of these traps serving their purpose to reduce the swarm's mobility.

But it's too soon to relax. The zombies are violently struggling against the rope; some are even trying to chomp and rip their way through. Most damning of all, they're plopping down off the castle walls faster than bubbles rising in roiling water. How long can rope last against these numbers?

"Men, use Lady Mizuha's holy water!"

Per Lex's orders, the knights throw the buckets of water onto the zombies. The rampaging zombies stop thrashing so vigorously, their movements slowing, becoming weaker. Their obnoxiously loud cries of

"SKRIEEE!" die down to moans of "Bwahhh."

"What a relief... It works even when they're souped-up."

The effect surpasses all expectations. I'm kind of torn to think they hate being doused in my spit that much, but it is what it is. Then again, someone who rejoices over being soaked in spit would be the wacky one, so their reaction isn't all that strange.

As I'm thinking about completely worthless stuff like that, my thoughts are interrupted by Lex's frantic shout.

"Lady Mizuha! May I ask you to purify them?!"

"You've got it!"

"I shall accompany you!"

The knights are using *sasumatas*—six-and-a-half-foot-long poles with wide U-shaped prongs on the end—to restrain the arms and torsos of the weakened zombies, pull them out of the rope, net, and snare traps, and hold them down on the ground. The scene is so brutal I nearly avert my eyes from it, but this is a necessary measure to bring the zombies back to the world of the living and to prevent others from becoming like them. Hardening my heart, I slap the restrained zombies as quickly as I can.

"Take this! And this! Hiyaah!"

"Well done!"

"Y-You think so? Ehehe." I was getting cocky because of Lex's praise, but I'm cruelly pulled back to reality when I see how many more zombies are still leaping down from the walls. "...Th-There are too many for me to purify."

"We already took that into consideration!" Lex tells me before turning to give orders to the knights. "Once you've restrained the weakened zombies, chuck them all into the underground aqueducts and pickle them in holy water!"

The knights line up the captured zombies on top of the rope net, tie it up, and drag the load behind them inside the castle. It's a creepy scene surpassing even surrealism.

"You can see what our plan is now. I apologize for the debased request, but I hope you can regularly provide us with saliva!"

"Start by doing something about the way you say it."

Bantering away like we usually do, we continue intercepting the endless swarm of zombies. Preparing for these turbo-charged ones in

## Another World's Zombie Apocalypse Is Not My Problem!

advance has paid off—time flows by without incident.

Occasionally, zombies chomp their way through the ropes or climb their way over others caught in the various traps below them, but quick action on the part of the knights suppresses them before any major damage can be done. About an hour has passed now.

"Lady Mizuha, how is your body faring…?"

"Taking a break earlier gave me enough energy to keep going for now."

Granted, I have much less energy than it sounds because of the fast speed and countless zombies I'm purifying nonstop. On the bright side, there's no threat of our line of defense being breached even in the event I'm rendered incapable of purifying. Moreover, the zombies scaling the walls have become more sporadic.

"Things look like they'll end well if we keep this up," I say, catching my breath.

I spoke too soon.

KABOOM! A bone-rattling, explosive sound shakes the ground. I jump and shudder.

"Whoa! What was that?!"

"The castle gates!"

Right after Lex's reply, the metal grates from the gate burst into the courtyard. A large figure looms in the gateway with nothing left to stop it.

"What the devil is that?!"

Torchlight reveals the massive figure to be a gigantic zombie! From top to bottom, it appears around fifteen feet tall, and abnormal muscle growth has given it enormous bulk! Between its swollen-beyond-recognition joints and protruding masses of flesh, it looks like a boneless ham. The complete lack of body hair is frankly revolting.

"GROAHHHHH!" Boneless Ham roars and charges. It's not the most agile zombie, but each step covers a lot of ground. In an instant, the zombie is upon the two closest knights, and it sends them flying with a sweep of its meaty right hand. The knights tumble and bounce off the ground several times until they finally lose momentum. They're barely moving—their injuries are serious.

"Get back!" Sir Oden orders, standing before the Boneless Ham with his trusty shield. "I'll take this monstrosity—" The words are knocked right out of his mouth as the Boneless Ham easily sends him flying with the same blow. Sir Oden slams into the wall and limply slides down.

"Captain!"

"Th-This can't be happening…!"

How could THAT Sir Oden be taken down in a single hit?! Reinfection is the least of our concerns now. Several of the knights are paralyzed in the face of certain death.

"Holy water! Hit it with holy water!"

One of the knights tosses a whole bucket of holy water on Boneless Ham. It squirms like a dog that's been sprayed with a hose, but that's it. It doesn't slow like the normal zombies.

"I-It doesn't work?!"

It's taller and wider than some houses. Maybe it simply needs to be hit with a much larger amount of holy water… Even if that's the case, it's near impossible to get close to the hulking thing without being knocked out. Most of the knights can't even get near the rampaging Boneless Ham.

"Hey…isn't this, like, really bad?"

"Yes, it is. To borrow your words, Lady Mizuha, we are frickin' doomed."

With how aggressively it's going berserk, I'll be squished into a pancake the second I go near it. No way can I purify that thing.

Grinding his teeth, Lex glowers at Boneless Ham. "Someone bring Lady Mizuha inside the tower keep!"

"What are you going to do, Lex?!"

"I will draw its attention. There is a serious threat of the ropes being destroyed if it continues its frenzy unchecked."

A sizeable army of zombies are still caught in the ropes beside the inner castle walls. If they get set loose, everyone, including the people sheltered inside the castle, will be devoured. But!

"It's way too reckless for you to take that thing on alone!"

"Even if my enemy is so large I must crane my neck to see it, or reeks so bad my nose is going to fall off…I, Lex Irvine, will not cower in fear!"

"Lex!"

Lex tosses his shield aside and runs at it with his sword drawn. Even he seems to have determined it not to be human as he swings his sword

# Another World's Zombie Apocalypse Is Not My Problem!

without mercy. But its skin is much thicker than anticipated and repels his sword with a clang.

"I-It's rock-solid!"

Boneless Ham is completely fixated on Lex now. After increasing the intensity of its growl, it begins dishing out repeated downward slams. Having tossed aside his shield in favor of lightness, Lex easily evades its attacks. At first glance, he seems to have a possibility of success, but the Boneless Ham's destructive strength is powerful enough to blow large holes into the ground with a single strike. He stands no chance if he's hit by that.

"Lex…!"

"Hurry, Lady Priestess, while Sir Lex is redirecting it."

The knight rushes me into the castle. I'm so worried about Lex, I keep looking over my shoulder. He's still dodging the attacks, but…I don't think he can keep it up until morning. Besides, we don't have any guarantee Boneless Ham will grow weaker in the sun.

Judging by its skin color and mutation, our opponent is definitely some form of zombie. Maybe defeating it is possible if I can just touch it, but that's a death wish with my level of athleticism. On the contrary: a bad move on my part could put Lex's life in danger too. Is there any way to stop it?

Clinging to the idea that I can do something, I sweep my eyes around the area until they land on an apple tree, and I'm struck with a thought. We might be able to injure the zombie if I can get a seed with my saliva on it to instantly mature into a full-grown tree right under its feet. Even if that doesn't stop it, it should inflict some damage.

But something is still lacking with this plan. After all, it's game over for me if I get hit once. I want to play any cards we have. First, we have to entrust planting the seed to someone agile—

"Oi! What're you doing?! It's dangerous out there! Get back inside!"

"Let go of me! Boss Lady is outside! Let go!"

I overhear a noisy argument the second I step into the castle. I quickly turn that way and see Rosso push his way past the knights.

"Rosso? What're you doing here?"

"Boss Lady! I was worried about you when I heard that explosion—Whoa, Boss Lady? Why do you look like you're about to make a life-changing gamble…?"

## Haru Yayari

I was just thinking about how he had shown up at the perfect time. He's nimble and quick enough to slip away from the knights. Nobody is more suitable for the job.

"Rosso, I have a favor to ask of you."

## ◆Chapter 14: Apparently, This Is What Happens When You Cram Meat Together

I move through the castle at a quick march with a group of twenty. Everyone is holding vases and buckets of various shapes and sizes. Inside each swirls water I have purified.

"Hard labor is outside my area of expertise…so why am I stuck partaking in this?" Pino grumbles as he walks beside me.

"No complaining. Look, even Cia is helping out."

"One, two, one, two." Cia is teetering unstably a few feet behind us.

"…What must be done must be done." Pino relents, unable to complain when he's compared with his country's young princess. Unwilling as he is, he ups his pace to a brisk trot. Striding alongside him, I peer into the bucket I'm holding against my chest with both hands.

"I wonder if the water will work."

"Didn't the zombie squirm from it?"

"Yeah, kinda cried out with an 'Ugyaaah' too."

"…In other words, we can assume that, while it has a higher resistance than normal zombies, holy water unmistakably affects it. No reason not to use it."

When I discussed my idea of how to defeat the Boneless Ham with Pino, he came up with a strategy based on it. The reason everyone is carrying around a large volume of water is to dump it on Boneless Ham.

At last, we arrive in the corridor facing the courtyard. All of a sudden, a bone-shuddering noise shakes the passage. Quickly, I look to see what happened outside the oriel window. Even now Lex is taking on Boneless Ham in the courtyard. He evades blows by rolling on the ground and springing to his feet. His movements no longer have the same composure and grace they did earlier.

"He's close to his limit," Pino warns.

"We have to hurry."

From the corridor just above the inner gate, an eaves-like scaffold protrudes over the courtyard. I step out onto that scaffolding with the others.

"Rosso, it's your turn!" I wave both hands at a corner of the courtyard. Rosso, who is on standby there, waves back.

He breaks into a run when he sees an opening in Boneless Ham's movement. He's as quick on his feet as ever. In the blink of an eye, he arrives in front of the inner gate.

Rosso quickly uses a shovel to dig a hole in the ground, plant the seed, and fill it with soil. He thrusts the shovel into the ground and grabs the wooden flask dangling from his waist.

"All set!"

With that signal, I lean over the scaffold and shout, "Lex, draw it toward Rosso!"

"You've got it, m'lady!"

Lex shouldn't know what it is we're trying to do, but he follows my command without questioning it. He slowly makes his way toward the inner gate while luring Boneless Ham and dodging its attacks.

"Rosso, I've brought you a friend!"

"Leave the rest to me, bro!"

Lex runs by Rosso with Boneless Ham hot on his tail. That hulking mass of muscle steps on the spot where the seed is buried, where Rosso had previously poured the holy water from his flask. Boneless Ham unleashes unsparing attacks without pause. Rosso nimbly evades them by diving to the side.

"Suck Boss Lady's enriching spit! Grow up big and strong, dear apples!"

Enriching spit? How the heck did he come up with that one? I'd love to lecture him on it for a whole day, but for now the entire area under Rosso's feet is brightly glowing. A sprout bursts from the ground, immediately flourishes into a full-grown apple tree, and powerfully lifts Boneless Ham off the ground.

# Another World's Zombie Apocalypse Is Not My Problem!

"HELL YEAH! That did the job!" Rosso exclaims, rejoicing.

Caught in the branches, Boneless Ham is having trouble moving. However, with its strength, the overpowered zombie breaks branch after branch. We don't have much time.

"Your Highness!" Pino instructs.

"Yes! Do it, everyone!"

At Cia's signal, everyone tosses the water on top of Boneless Ham. Each bucket didn't have that much water on its own, but combined, it's a fair amount. Soaked with no spot on its enormous body left untouched, Boneless Ham writhes in agony.

"GWRAAHHH…!"

"It's working!"

Sadly, the apple tree can't withstand Boneless Ham's excessive weight. Creaking, it finally snaps. Boneless Ham rolls onto the ground. Affected by the water, it lies there limp.

"Miss Priestess," Pino bellows as if he was waiting for this moment, "purify it now!"

"All right! Leave it to me! …Uh, hold on! How exactly am I supposed to get down from here?"

"The answer is obvious. Jump."

"…Excuse me?"

Pino, the boy who had been stone-faced until now, flashes a killer smirk—the kind that literally kills, because he just shoved me off the freaking ledge. My hands dog-paddle through the air to grab hold of the scaffolding ledge in vain. My whole body is plummeting toward the courtyard.

"NO! You little jerk! Is this some kinda sick joke?!" I scream as I fall.

"Do your job, Miss Priestess."

"Big Sister!" Cia, unlike the ruthless jerk Pino, reaches for me. But I'll drag her down with me if I take her hand.

*You'd better remember what you did here, Pino, because I'm coming for you later!* Resentfully cursing him, I prepare myself for the inevitable.

"Sir Lex, a lady is falling from the sky!"

"L-Lady Mizuha?!"

"I-I'M COUNTING ON YOUUUUUU!"

My flight time is brief. Lex catches me. He's holding me princess-style, but there's not even a molecule of a sweet, romantic mood in the air. On the contrary, Lex's face is so strained the veins are popping from his face.

"NNGHHH!"

"I'm not heavy, am I?"

"O-Of course you are light, m'lady!"

"You pass with *flying* colors. Anyway, thanks!"

I wrap up that conversation with Lex within a few seconds and leap from his arms. When I get closer to the weakened Boneless Ham, its excessively protruding muscles and bloody veins are graphically defined. Frankly, it's so disgusting it's making me physically sick. Having to touch this thing makes me want to cry, but doing that is the only option.

I'm finally close enough that my hand should reach it. Enduring the rancid stench, I stretch out my arm as far as it can go, but before I make contact, Boneless Ham's pure-muscle left arm swells. Regaining its agility, it sends a left-hand thrust my way.

Uh, is this really happening?! I'll break—bones and all—if that boulder-sized fist hits me. It'll be end of story. End of the line.

Just as I'm preparing for my last moments, Boneless Ham's fist is flung upward as if repelled by something. What in the world just happened? The answer is right in front of me: the bloodied knight who leaped in front of me—Sir Oden—deflected the punch with that big shield of his.

"Sir Oden!"

"Do it now, Lady Mizuha!"

Spurred on by his desperate cry, I kick off and slap the staggering Boneless Ham's belly.

"YICK," I can't help whimpering at the sticky, jellylike feeling under my hand as Boneless Ham's body begins emitting light.

Puzzle piece–like seams emerge on the figure, and from there, the body falls apart like droplets of water. By the time the light fades, Boneless Ham is gone. In its place is a large number of—

"A-Animals?"

Cows, deer, and pigs have fallen out of the seams onto the ground. Though they seem to be unconscious, every animal is alive and breathing. I know I was calling that thing Boneless Ham like the meat…but to think it really was made up of animals. I don't think I can eat another ham… On the other hand, I'm personally more surprised to see animals I recognize. It's probably because we already defeated it, but a part of me wishes Boneless Ham had actually been more of a horror creature.

## Another World's Zombie Apocalypse Is Not My Problem!

"Vianta!" Lex pushes his way into the herd of fallen animals. It sounds like his beloved horse is in the mix. Vianta, the chestnut horse lying on her side, opens her big brown eyes as Lex strokes her muzzle. She nuzzles his face, rejoicing in their reunion.

"So Vianta was in there too. I'm glad you found her."

"Me too! I have you to thank for that, Lady Mizuha. Truly, I can never thank you enough…!"

She must be like family to Lex. I'm enjoying the happy moment, except it's ruined by the chorus of "Bwahhh bwahhh" around us. I was so caught up in defeating Boneless Ham that I'd forgotten about the town's worth of zombies still ensnared in the ropes.

"Their purification can be saved for another day. As the Goddess's blessing has it, continuing to douse them with water renders them containable," Sir Oden suggests, standing at my side.

Holding off until another day takes a big load off my shoulders. I'm pretty positive I'll pass out if I tried to purify now. But we have other things to be more concerned about at the moment. Such as the blood spurting from Sir Oden's head.

"Sir Oden, thank you for saving me. Are you all right? You are bleeding—"

"Ha! I wouldn't be the captain of the knights if I collapsed from this puny blood loss— Blurgh!"

"Hey?! Sir Oden?! You look like you've sustained some serious injuries, though!" I cry out, flustered.

"Just kidding," he guffaws, giving me thumbs-up.

Is he really okay? Chances are high he's just pretending to be fine, so I want him seen by a doctor as soon as possible.

I take another look around the destroyed courtyard. Unfortunately, not everyone got by unscathed. If nothing else, though, we will see the morning alive and unzombified.

## ◆Chapter 15: Signs of a Way Home

**TEN** days have passed since the night of the black fog that brought Boneless Ham. I spent most of that time purifying the zombies flocking around the outer wall. There were so many I was starting to get fed up with doing it every single day, but that mission just ended a few moments ago. Grantz Kingdom is finally on the way to revitalization.

"I. Am. BEAT! Can't move anymore."

We're in the outermost sector of the capital city. I plop down on the cobblestones near the castle gate. It's improper to sit on the dirty ground in the middle of the road, but I couldn't care in the least right now. Exhaustion ten times worse than ever before presses down on me—perhaps from the relief I won't have to purify anything for a while.

Lots of people are walking around the city already. Reactions to the state of things vary from those who are debilitated by depression over their destroyed homes and those who quickly set about making repairs. As I watch them from the road, I'm struck by a sudden question.

"Hey, do you have enough building materials?"

"As you rightly guessed, we do not. We are especially lacking in wood," Lex answers from where he stands attentively at my side.

"I wonder if we can use the apple trees."

"Apple trees don't make for good lumber, so the most it could be used for is smaller items," Lex explains, shifting his gaze beyond the walls. "In any event, we have little choice but to set up an expeditionary squad to harvest trees."

"You want to harvest the trees? Uh, aren't they rotten everywhere?"

## Another World's Zombie Apocalypse Is Not My Problem!

"Indeed. For that reason, may I request your saliv— AHEM! Your holy water, Lady Mizuha?!"

"You were just about to ask for my saliva again, weren't you?"

"Never. I asked for your holy water, Lady Mizuha."

Putting it that way sounds just as bad. On the flip side, digging in my heels about it is just going to make it worse for me, so I'm leaving it at that.

"Well, whatever. I plan to help out where I can if it's for the sake of rebuilding."

"Thank you very much. I wholeheartedly rejoice that you are who you are, Lady Mizuha."

"...Let me be clear: I'm only helping out because I want a safe place to sleep and bathe. I still view this as your problem, not mine. I'm not the saint you think I am, Lex."

"For your benefit, we shall leave it at that."

"Grr! There you go again, deflecting what I'm saying!"

Things will just get too constrained for me if they expect too much of me as a "do-gooder." I'm speaking from my experience as "Class Rep Mizuha" in elementary school. Just because I was the class representative they took advantage of me, saying things like "You can solve this problem" and "You can eat the school lunch without leaving anything on your plate" and "The teachers can leave you to watch over the class while they're away."

To this day, it's still a huge mystery to me how following my brother's cryptic advice to stop wearing my hair in braids actually freed me from the hell of being picked as class representative. When it all comes down to it, I just want to live in comfort. That's my true reason for helping them with their zombie problem.

"Boss Lady!"

I look toward the main road where I heard that shout and find Rosso waving at me. The second he's standing in front of me, he slams his hands on his knees and drops into a deep bow.

"Thank you for working hard at your duties today!"

"Didn't I tell you to lay off that greeting?"

I hate feeling like he's aged me to a working adult.

"Why?! Doesn't it sound cool?!"

"When I say no, I mean no."

"Yes, ma'am."

We've repeated this same conversation five times already. He hasn't stopped yet, so it's a given he'll keep it up.

I sigh and ask him why he's here: "So? What's up? You must have a reason to come all this way."

Given how annoyingly huge the capital city is, you work up a sweat coming to the outer castle wall. It's hard to imagine him making the trek out here for nothing.

"Right, right. I do. That tiny scholar Pino entrusted me with a message for you."

"Pino did? What did he say?"

"He said, 'Come to the Royal Library to discuss *that* matter,'" Rosso relays, imitating Pino. I'll keep it to myself that he doesn't sound a thing like him.

"That matter" must be our discussion about the other world. I'd completely forgotten his promise to tell me about it once I'd liberated Grantz's capital city from zombies.

"Thanks for the message, Rosso."

"Don't mention it. Anything for you, Boss Lady."

At first, I had a tough time getting used to Rosso, a guy who looks just like a small-time villain, idolizing me, but now it seems so natural. I'm startled by my ability to easily adapt to these things.

"M'kay, I'm off to see Pino. See you two later," I say in parting and run off, only to skid to a halt a second later. I look over my shoulder and ask, "Uh, where is the Royal Library?"

**THE** Royal Library was constructed near the castle. It looks like a stone tower on the outside. Though shorter than the castle, it's the second tallest structure. My curiosity about what this building was has finally been sated after all this time.

I part ways with Rosso, who showed me the way here, at the entrance and go inside. I swing my inquisitive gaze around the building while Pino, who met me at the entrance, leads the way.

"Wow! This is my first time inside such a huge library…"

Innumerable bookshelves line the walls. The atrium structure allows

## Another World's Zombie Apocalypse Is Not My Problem!

you to see the upper stories from below, and every floor is filled to capacity with bookshelves. Sadly, the interior is constructed from wood, which rotted with the zombie blight. Because of that, I have to watch my step as the floorboards occasionally give way.

"This was normally a place of tranquility, but you can see the deplorable state it's in now."

"Do you think I can purify it?"

"Doesn't hurt to try."

With that decided, I spit on a nearby bookshelf while mentally asking for every librarian in the universe to forgive me. After the bookshelf glows, it regains its former glory. That test proves I can purify the books, but...

"Geh! It only did one shelf!"

I'd imagined the holy light spreading through the library, purifying the whole thing like with water, but things never go as easy as I hope they will.

"In conclusion, we can bring the library back if you spit on every bookshelf," Pino states like the concluding paragraph of a research paper.

"Not happening."

"I thought so."

"I mean, it's not like I can't do it, but I don't even want to imagine myself doing it, much less actually commit the act..."

Just from what I can see, there are more than a hundred bookshelves. In what world can you find a high school girl going around spitting on over a hundred bookshelves in a library? I don't think there's any person, let alone high school girls, who would do that. In no way do I want to cross that line into irredeemable weirdo-freak territory.

"Well, I don't think we should rely on you for everything, Miss Priestess."

"You really are the Grantz Kingdom's conscience, Pino..."

"I simply want to prevent this country from stagnating."

"Aw, there you go being modest. Want me to pat you on the head and tell you what a good little boy you are?"

"Don't treat me like a child!"

As we're having that conversation, we arrive at the reading space prepared in a corner of the first floor. We find a suitable table and sit facing each other.

"Time to begin our discussion."

"Please teach me, Professor Pino."

"…What's with that form of address?"

"You're going to teach me stuff, so I figured I might as well act like a student."

"Please act normal."

He sounds fed up with me. Darn.

Pino clears his throat and begins his lecture. "About this world… is where I'd like to start, but you should learn the basics about our god first. After all, you don't seem to know anything about this world, Miss Priestess."

"You are indeed correct, Professor," I say with teasing formality before switching back to casual dialogue. "Say, is that god the same as the goddess Lex and the others talk about?"

"They are one and the same. God of love. God of fertility. The names vary throughout the lands, but they all apply to the same deity: Goddess Sadia. The being who created this world."

"Goddess Sadia…" I repeat her name, but it doesn't mean anything to me.

"However, the Goddess didn't create the world from nothingness. Word has it that she created this one based on her own. This is lore from the beginning of time when the Goddess supposedly spoke with man."

"It'd be reasonable for me to think of the world the Goddess is from as 'another world,' right? Do you know what that one was like?"

Pino laughs dryly like I'm a lost cause when I immediately latch on to the mention of another world. "Of course. I assume there are similarities between the two because the other world was the basis for ours. I have no doubt it's more developed than this one too."

"Hmm. Mine is definitely further along than this world, and there are a lot of similarities… Like the food, animals, and buildings."

Obviously, there weren't any zombies…unless people without caffeine count.

"Do you know anything else?"

"Regrettably, this is it. I'm sorry to have deceived you, but as you just heard, all I have is conjecture."

Apparently, he has only this obscure information. "Ugghh," I groan.

## Another World's Zombie Apocalypse Is Not My Problem!

Pino folds his arms in front of his chest as he reclines against the back of his chair. "That being said, I believe it isn't necessary for your world and the Goddess's world to be one and the same for you to go home."

"H-How so?"

"I sincerely doubt anyone aside from the Goddess is capable of the extraordinary feat of bringing someone here from another world."

"You mean she summoned me here? For what purpose?"

"Ask the Goddess. The one thing I can say for sure is that she has the ability to connect this world to others. You don't have to lose hope if you know that much, no?"

Using Pino's hint, I voice my conclusion. "In other words, there's a chance I can return to my world if I meet this goddess?"

"There you have it. Even if you can't go straight home, that should take you one step closer to it."

"But is a goddess someone you can meet? You can't meet gods and goddesses in my world."

Regardless of whether deities actually exist, gods visible to the public don't exist in my world. There are beings who are worshipped like gods, but naturally none of them possess the power to create the heavens and the earth like this world's goddess.

"For what it's worth, I haven't met her," Pino says dully, resting his chin in his hands. "Accounts of people beholding the Goddess can be found in old texts, but their authenticity is up for debate. And let's face it—the world has literally gone to hell. What is our goddess doing, then? It's reasonable to assume she's not here right now."

"Seriously? Then what am I supposed to—"

"Don't panic just yet. I've already thought about that." Here it is again—Pino's killer smirk. "You see, there's this theory that the Goddess and the Dark Djinn are opposite sides of the same existence. The basis for this lies in their power. The Dark Djinn's power to corrupt everything stands in direct contrast to the Goddess's power to purify everything."

"You're right... They are polar opposites."

"See? So when you apply that theory to my idea that she 'isn't here right now'...it leads to but one conclusion."

"Oh! I know what it is!" I think I have the right idea, but I'll run it by him to be sure. "Let's see... There's a single entity called God, and while Goddess Sadia is in control, the Dark Djinn sleeps. Then when the Dark Djinn is in control, the Goddess is asleep... Does that fit?"

"Correct. So, what do you think we should do based on that information?"

"If the Dark Djinn is also the Goddess, we just have to meet the Dark Djinn to find her. Uhh, but doesn't that bring us back to the beginning? We don't know where the Dark Djinn is either."

"Unlike the Goddess, we actually have information on the Dark Djinn, you know?"

I can't remember ever hearing anything about where the Dark Djinn is. But Pino is acting like I should know. In other words, I've obtained the information along the way without realizing it. The Dark Djinn is the god of evil, so he should be the symbol of evil things.

"The zombies?"

"Wrong."

"The rotten earth?"

"Wrong."

"Grr..." I childishly puff out my cheeks. I can think of only one more possibility. "...How about the black fog?"

"Correct. Though I had expected you to get it on your first try."

"Sorry that I suck at guessing."

"Don't pout. I wouldn't call this an apology, but I've already located the source of the black fog, based on the information you provided me before."

"I knew I could count on you, Pino!"

Exasperated with how fast I bounced back, Pino spreads a map out on the table. "Take a look at this. The black fog has shown up in two spots. First, on the highway leading to the capital. Second, Grantz Castle. The black fog moved the short distance between these two locations. You can find the origin by following its course."

Pino's small finger traces the line drawn from Grantz Castle until it eventually intersects with the line extending from the highway. The intersection point is right where a forest is drawn on the map.

"Are you suggesting the Dark Djinn is around there?"

"If we leave out the unanswered question of whether the black fog only travels in a straight path."

# Another World's Zombie Apocalypse Is Not My Problem!

"This is a case of 'it doesn't hurt to look,' huh?"

"Exactly. In addition, we don't know for sure if the Dark Djinn itself is there. But you are very likely to find information relating to it." We're groping for clues at this point. Anything that can be tested should be tested.

"I'll investigate into the matter for you. It's a given the knights will jump at the chance to help you if I throw your name out. Even if they have to slobber all over themselves to do it."

"Slobber all over themselves...?"

"Oh, my bad. It's our holy priestess who slobbers," Pino says with a smirk. "Whoa. Down, girl. I'm sorry for joking around! So please put that chair back down."

"You should be sorry!" I grumble as I place the chair on the floor. Taking my seat again, I run another one of my questions by him. "But wait, aren't we forgetting something important. Even if we find this Dark Djinn, Goddess Sadia is supposedly asleep. What do I do when I find it?"

"The answer is right there, no?"

I follow Pino's gaze to my right hand resting on top of the table. "My hand?"

"It has the power to remove the Dark Djinn's curse. Maybe it's capable of giving control back to the Goddess."

"Hmm... I wonder if that's really possible."

"We literally have no other hand to play. I, at least, believe it's worth a shot."

What form has the Dark Djinn taken? What kind of powers does it have? Not even being able to imagine it makes me uneasy, but nothing will happen if I don't act.

"I see what you mean... Okay, I'll try it."

"Understood. Then I'll expect you to move according to that plan. I'll contact you once I finish my investigation. Feel free to do what you want until then." Pino stands and walks toward the door before he finishes talking. "I'll be taking my leave now."

"Aw, you're leaving already?"

"I have to, because a certain someone has just stuck me with a ton of work." He doesn't look like he hates that as much as he makes it sound. Maybe he's excited as a scholar to learn more about the Goddess and the Dark Djinn.

"Pino, thanks for everything!"

"Don't worry about it. This is a cheap price to pay to thank you for saving my country." Pino waves at me over his shoulder.

I watch his tiny back leave the library, thinking how mature he is for his age.

**Another World's Zombie Apocalypse Is Not My Problem!**

◆Chapter 16: My Goddess

**TODAY,** like every day, is just another day of zombie purifying. On the bright side, the zombies flocking around the outer walls have been fully taken care of, which makes purifying the outlying area my primary duty now. I've also grown crops with my spit, but I consider that a part of my dark past never to be mentioned again.

"By the way, I heard everyone has been sent back to their homes. Is that smart?"

It's a nice and warm, sunny afternoon. I'm walking down the capital's main street with Lex, watching the people rebuilding the city.

"Won't zombies come bwahhing at their door if they make too much noise? I've purified most of the zombies in the general area, but in a zombie apocalypse, you can never be too cautious."

"As you feared, the outer walls are still too dangerous. Our countermeasure has been making that area off-limits to all but the knights regardless of the time of day. I feel sorry for residents of the affected regions, but we have moved them into alternative housing for the time being."

"They just have to put up with it, huh? What with the straggler zombies we run into now and then."

All the zombies in the area were supposed to have been taken care of yesterday, and yet several dozen more were discovered this morning. They must have migrated during the night.

"We have a long ways to go before we can relax. Orders have gone out to the citizens to stay as quiet as possible at night just in case."

"I get the feeling a lot more households are going to start telling their children that zombies are going to come for them if they don't go to bed."

"Z-Zombies realistically might show up, giving weight to that threat..."

I can tolerate zombies because of all I've been through, but their appearance is downright horrifying. If I had seen their gruesome faces as a child, I would've been traumatized for sure.

"Anyhoo, I just don't know what to do with all my sudden free time."

"Are you speaking of the matter you requested of Sir Pino? I heard of it from the Royal Knights. What a brave lady you are, volunteering to embark on a journey to defeat the Dark Djinn in order to save the world ..."

Ahh. That's the story he told? This must be Pino's clever way of spurring people to action when few would believe the fishy story about my being from another world and wanting to go home.

"A pure and beautiful heart that thinks of the people's safety above all else—as to be expected of you, Lady Mizuha."

"K-Knock it off. I keep telling you I'm not like that."

Of course, I hope the people of this world can live in peace as a result, but I can't tell them my desire to return home is the driving factor.

"Please allow me to accompany you in subjugating the Dark Djinn. I, Lex Irvine, swear to be of use to you."

"Sure. I'll ask you to come along when the time comes."

"Thank you, m'lady!" Brimming with confidence, Lex taps his fist against his chest.

A loud clatter suddenly echoes from somewhere nearby. I whip my eyes toward where lumber has fallen and scattered in front of a house. A little boy is crouched on the ground holding his leg.

"Are you okay?!"

"It hurts! It huuuurts!"

I dash over to the boy. Leaning over, I examine his leg. He hit his knee, though the injury isn't too severe. He seems to have tripped over the squared lumber and landed on his knees. Blood is oozing from the scrape. We need to disinfect it fast.

"Lex, can you bring me water?"

"Yes, m'lady! I will be right back with it!"

## Another World's Zombie Apocalypse Is Not My Problem!

The boy probably doesn't want his scrape rinsed with water cleansed by spit, but he'll just have to bear with it. If my powers have stuck me with the cliché priestess title, the least they could do is heal injuries.

A split second after that thought, faint light emits briefly from my left hand placed on the boy's leg.

"...That's weird... It doesn't hurt..." The boy is calm and quiet, as if his tears had been fake. I blink several times, but not because the boy suddenly stopped crying.

"The scrape healed...?"

The bleeding cut on the boy's knee has cleanly vanished. I know I was thinking it'd be great if I could heal, but I didn't think it'd actually happen. In retrospect, I've been smacking people with my right hand all this time and barely touching others with my left. As far as I can remember, I haven't touched a single injured person with my left hand.

"I've been looking everywhere for you, Lyle. Oh dear. Why are you sitting in a place like that?"

"Ah, Mommy! I tripped over those logs and fell."

"You fell? Are you all right? Did you hurt yourself?"

"I was bleeding, but this nice lady healed me." The boy, Lyle, points at me.

"She healed you...?" The mother turns a suspicious eye on me.

I've read and watched plenty of stories where people freak out when someone heals others with a mysterious power. People are already gathering around us. Gazes are burrowing into me from all directions. This can't be good.

"I-If you will excuse me..."

"Wait just a moment."

I had spun around and was about to make a quick escape, but they called me to a stop. I fearfully turn back. "Wh-What is it?"

"Thank you. How can I ever thank you enough? Lyle, thank the nice lady too."

"I know. Thanks, lady!"

I'm thrown off balance by their unexpected reaction. But suddenly becoming aware of how extremely suspicious I'm acting, I quickly muster my composure to respond in kind.

"M-My pleasure. I didn't do much."

Even though I say that, viewed objectively, healing a wound in an instant is doing a lot. The onlookers seem to think so, too, as they continue regarding me with skepticism. Lex returns with a jar of water around the time a slight commotion starts to break out.

"Lady Mizuha? What is going on here?"

"Oh, Lex. Uh, I seemed to have instantly healed this child's wounds with my left hand."

"I see."

"You aren't surprised?"

"No, m'lady."

What a fast answer. I seriously don't understand Lex's sensibility. But I'm about to.

"After all, Lady Mizuha is the holy priestess! Healing an injury or two is only natural for you!"

"What the heck is with that nonsense reason?! And would you please lower your voice?!"

Thanks to Lex's big mouth, surprised chatter rises from the crowd.

"He said she's the priestess."

"That lady is the priestess?"

Oh my gosh. What I've been fearing all along has come true! It won't be long now before they snort, "This pitiful woman is the priestess? Pft!"

As I'm holding my aching head, a voice rings out like a flash of lightning in the sky: "No! You are incorrect!"

Searching for whoever said that, my gaze lands on a young woman clad in what looks exactly like the distinctive habit worn by Catholic nuns. The woman, with her well-defined facial features and violet eyes, is enchantingly beautiful even by my standards. Silver hair peeks out of her veil.

"She is not the priestess," the nunlike woman declares, then continues in an authoritative voice, "She is the Goddess!"

IN a corner of the castle's third floor, I'm enjoying tea with Cia in an inner garden with a beautiful view outside. Naturally, a luxury item such as tea leaves could be prepared only with *that* method. It's a little late for it now, but when I think about the process needing something from

# Another World's Zombie Apocalypse Is Not My Problem!

inside my body, I can only say I have complicated feelings. It's best not to think about it at all.

"Big Sis, you look unwell," Cia comments, her voice laced with worry.

To be perfectly honest, I've been hoping she would ask why I'm so out of it so I could complain.

"Listen to this! Someone showed up while I was patrolling the city during lunch and proclaimed, 'She's not the priestess. She's the Goddess!'"

"G-Goddess... That's a new one..."

"Right? Calling me Goddess is taking it a step too far. *Priestess* is already awful enough."

That nunlike woman had continued shouting "Goddess! My goddess!" after that. Things took a turn for the worse when she began preaching and insisting to the crowd that I'm the Goddess. Lex and the knights who ran over to assist were able to get the situation under control, but I felt like burying my head in the sand the whole time... Ugh, my stomach hurts just thinking about it.

"But why *goddess* of all things?"

"Yeah, that had to do with this kid who happened to fall and hurt himself. When I placed my left hand on the injury, it fully recovered in an instant."

"B-Big Sister Goddess!"

"Don't you start too, Cia!"

"I was joking," she giggles, then adds, "And half-serious."

Is it just me or does she look completely serious, not just half? Please let it be just me.

"However, it isn't unreasonable for this woman to believe you are the Goddess, for you have the exact same powers the Goddess is said to have in myths."

Now that she mentions it, Pino also said the Goddess has the power to purify. If the power to heal is included with that, then it makes the claim more credible. But—

"Just so you know, that isn't me, okay? I'm not your goddess or your priestess."

"Yes, your Cia knows this," Cia responds with an ear-to-ear grin. This is that same playing-along-with-it face from before.

When people get like this, whatever I say just falls flat, so all I can do is sigh. Anyway, they sure are working fast at strengthening the outer moat from what I can see outside. My thoughts on the matter are interrupted by the clang of armored footsteps. I look that way and see Lex standing in the pillared corridor facing the garden.

"Pardon the interruption, ladies. May I borrow a moment of your time?"

"Yes, I do not mind. How about you, Big Sis?"

"Go right ahead."

Lex descends into the garden with my unenthusiastic approval.

"Lady Mizuha, I investigated that woman."

"That woman? You mean the one who kicked up the goddess fuss this afternoon?"

"Yes," Lex affirms. "Her name is Iris. She appears to have been raised in an orphanage located in a village not far from the capital."

"In an orphanage?"

"Indeed. Regrettably, that orphanage went under by the time she was twelve due to financial difficulties coupled with not receiving government aid."

I don't know how to respond. Losing the place where you grew up must have been a terrible shock to her.

"She has lived in a church located in the capital ever since, but whether it stems from the orphanage shutting down or not, she often has crazy bursts of activity, causing constant problems under the banner of it being God's will. This time is no exception, for she has...well... started the Church of Our Lady Mizuha."

"That's my name!"

I like my name, but there is no more humiliating way for a name to be used than to have it turned into a religious cult! Couldn't she have come up with something a little more, I don't know, creative?

"H-Has anyone joined yet?"

"No, not one. If anything, they seem to be avoiding it like the zombie curse."

"I'm the biggest victim of this atrocity."

It totally makes sense that people wouldn't join such a dubious cult, but...I seriously feel like my ego just took a major hit.

"There is one major concern, though. The people of this kingdom worship Goddess Sadia, and among their ranks are extremist religious

## Another World's Zombie Apocalypse Is Not My Problem!

fanatics. Iris may be in danger if they view her actions as sacrilege against the Goddess."

"A-Are they really dangerous people?"

"I understand they turn people to stone and decorate them as goddess statues..."

"Yeah, okay, that's dangerous." Iris is the epitome of a weirdo, but I don't want to see her put in danger. "How do we handle this one?" I groan.

Cia springs to her feet. "We can't leave this matter unattended if we consider the anxiety it causes Big Sister. Lex, please keep track of the movements taken by both parties. Apprehend them if they go too far."

"As you command, Your Highness."

Things seem to be taking a violent turn.

"Please don't get too rough—"

"No. This is the time to bring down the hammer. It is a good opportunity to show one and all what happens when they cause problems for you, Big Sis. Now go, Lex!" Cia orders in a frigidly firm voice, thrusting her finger in the direction of the city.

*Um, cute little Cia? Did your personality just change?*

## ◆Chapter 17: Believer Coalescence

**BY** noon the next day, I've finished purifying wandering zombies and blighted land in the area, and have returned to the capital city with Lex. One of the knights recognizes Lex from a distance and runs over to us.

"Sir Lex!"

"Please excuse me, Lady Mizuha." Lex and the knight begin discussing something while they stand a few feet away. Both of their faces are grim. The conversation wraps up quickly, and Lex returns to my side.

"Something to do with Iris?"

"You could tell?"

"Well, yeah, after what went down yesterday. Things aren't going well?"

"The Goddess Sadia Fanatics are a single group, so their discovery is easy. Iris, however, has hidden her whereabouts since the incident yesterday."

"She hasn't been captured by the fanatics, has she?"

"Their base of operations is being monitored even now, and I have not received any report of her capture."

"She's safe for now, then." I exhale a sigh of relief.

Lex turns a dazzling smile on me. "You truly are kind, Lady Mizuha."

"Nah. I'm not. I just don't want her stirring up trouble using my name."

She's the wacko who started a new religion in my name. If something bad happens, not only will it weigh heavily on my conscience, it'll haunt

### Another World's Zombie Apocalypse Is Not My Problem!

me for the rest of my life.

"But I wonder where she went."

"Many buildings are still vacant, so we will just have to search for her at random."

"Sorry about this. I feel bad this happened because of me."

"This is simply another knightly duty." Lex beams with pride.

"Fight! A fight has broken out down the road!" someone shouts.

What the heck are these people doing in the midst of the apocalypse?! I exchange looks with Lex.

"Lex!"

"Yes, let's check it out!"

It's great and all that we broke into a run together, but as soon as my left foot hits the ground, I stagger. Fatigue from using my power all morning long hasn't lifted yet.

"L-Lady Mizuha?!" Lex turns back for me. "Are you all right?"

"Sorry! I'm more exhausted than I thought from this morning. Go ahead without me."

"...As you wish, m'lady!"

I watch Lex reluctantly run in the direction of the fight. I feel guilty, but I'll leave settling it to him and take this time to rest. Besides, it's not like I can do much by going with him. At best, I can heal any injuries caused by the brawl.

I'm leaning against the wall of the nearest house when all of a sudden everything goes dark. For a second, I wonder what happened, but then it instantly clicks that someone's pulled a bag over my head.

"H-Hey?! What are you doing?! What's the big idea?!" I paw at the bag with little effect beyond it stretching slightly. I struggle frantically anyway until I'm suddenly wrapped in a hug that pins my hands down. From the feel of it, this has to be another person's body. And they're restraining me with only one arm, yet they're so strong I can't shake them.

"I want to avoid hurting you if possible, so please don't struggle."

"That voice... Are you possibly Iris?"

"You remember me?! I am deeply honored, Goddess!"

Her clear voice oozes a saccharine sweetness that disturbs me. Strangely enough, feeling unsettled helps me regain my head. I timorously ask a question to get a better grasp on the situation.

"…What are you after?"

"Your servant Iris simply came to return the Goddess to her rightful place."

My feet are lifted off the ground. Apparently, she just hefted me onto her shoulder. I thought she had a fragile, delicate body, but boy does it house some inhuman strength. This is probably not the time to put up a fuss.

Iris secures me on her shoulder like a sack of potatoes and starts running. After five minutes of hearing her panting heavily in my ear like a dog, I'm finally freed from the bag.

I'm in a dark room about 130 square feet large. I have partial visibility from the sunlight filtering in through the window covered with an old rag.

"Where is this place…?"

"The holy headquarters of the Church of Our Lady Mizuha!"

A rather shabby location for such a lofty name. Iris had tied my arms and legs to a chair and placed me in the dead center of the room. She takes a great big breath and buries her face in my chest. Rubbing her face hard against me, she begins noisily snorting my scent like some kind of dog.

"Goddess! Goddess!"

"Wh-What the heck are you doing?! Stop it! Quit it!"

"Gentle and warm like the sun… This is my goddess's smell! Iris has it memorized now!"

I have never been smelled like this by someone before. My face is burning with humiliation. Iris finally pries her face from my chest, only to wrap her arms around my lap and start nuzzling me there.

…What is this woman's problem?!

"Um, Iris? Why are you doing this?" I ask, trying my best to keep my voice calm.

"Doing what?"

"Confining me here, for starters…"

"This isn't confinement. It is the natural order for Goddess Mizuha to be enshrined and worshipped at the Church of Our Lady Mizuha."

Uhh, I can't tell if we're on the same page or not.

"When the world decayed, I thought the goddess I believed in had betrayed me. But she did not betray. She has descended from the heavens in human form to save the world!"

"Yeaahh, I'm a normal human."

"No, you are the Goddess! Goddess Sadia was Goddess Mizuha all along!"

Nothing she says makes sense, but I now know she still mistakenly views me as the deity of this world. At any rate, I want to get out of here.

Lex said he didn't know where Iris was hiding—he probably won't be coming to save me anytime soon. In which case, I have to break out of here by myself. Even though I hate playing into this madness, pretending to be Iris's goddess should help me escape.

"Um, Iris? Would you mind undoing these ropes? My skin hurts from them cutting into me…"

"No can do. You're planning to run away, aren't you?"

"N-No, I'm not. I won't run away, okay?"

Holding back my twitching cheeks, I continue forcing my best smile through. Iris, however, stares hard at my face. I can tell she's on guard. If only I could think of a way to make releasing me beneficial to her…

"I just wanted you to unbind me so I can pat you on the head. Haha."

That was a horrible excuse, if I do say so myself.

## Another World's Zombie Apocalypse Is Not My Problem!

"Very well."

Seriously? She was convinced by that? She really is like a big dog.

"But please make it three pats on the head. And make them full-circle pats."

"S-Sure."

Is she cheeky or what? At any rate, I accept her conditions because she's not asking for much. She quickly unties the rope. I'm finally free, but my liberation is short-lived. Since nothing about my current predicament has changed, my nerves are still on edge.

Iris lightly crouches in front of me and offers her head. "Okay, Goddess, please do what you promised."

"O-Okay, I'll do it."

I cautiously begin patting her on the head. I'm touching her veil, so I have no particular comment on the feel. Eventually, I fulfill her request for three full-circle pats. Iris enters a prayer pose, smiling in ecstasy.

"Aah. I never believed the blessed day would arrive when the Goddess would pat me on the head... Supreme bliss!"

While Iris is in a state of rapture, I stealthily sneak away, breaking into an all-out run. Just a little farther and I'll reach the door! And that's when she firmly seizes hold of my arm.

"You promised you wouldn't run away. You deceived me," Iris whispers in a low, deadly voice over my shoulder.

"L-Listen, I really have to pee! That's why!"

"A goddess should not lie." She spins me around to face her and brings her emotionless face right up to mine. Her beautiful features make it all the scarier. "Please use that if you need the restroom." She points to a wine barrel. It doesn't even pass for a chamber pot.

"No, no, no, no. I can't use that—"

"You will be living out the rest of your life here. If you can't do your business there, you are welcome to use the floor." Her voice is dispassionate but incredibly intimidating. This woman is dead serious.

"Your holy headquarters are going to stink."

"I fully welcome anything that comes from the Goddess."

"And I am fully repulsed..."

I can't believe she is this infatuated with me. It'd be kind of cute if she listened to anything I said, but to my grave misfortune, she's not that type.

"Come along now, Goddess Mizuha. Return to your shrine…" Iris leads me back to the center of the room by the hand.

The Royal Knights are actively searching for Iris's whereabouts, but the capital city is large and complex. If worst comes to worst, I'll be living in captivity for a long time. The silver lining in this whole mess is that I won't be killed or tortured, but not even I'm optimistic enough to withstand being confined to this dank room forever.

If only Lex could come to my rescue like before. My hopeful thoughts are disrupted by the cracking sound of wood being smashed to pieces. I look over my shoulder at the damaged door. Did Lex really come for me?

That hope is dashed a second later, when three unfamiliar men barge into the room through the broken door. All three are clad in dull navy religious habits consisting of a tunic covered by a scapular and cowl.

"Sadia Fanatics, I presume?" Iris snarls, glaring at the men.

It appears these men are members of the Goddess Sadia Fanatics Lex told me about. They seem to have some sort of close connection to Iris.

"Stop calling us fanatics. We simply have a stronger faith in Goddess Sadia than other believers."

"Excessive faith only makes you blind."

*You're the last person I want to hear that from, Iris.*

"You have deified that woman and blasphemed Goddess Sadia. These actions are unforgivable. We will now purge you as a heretic."

The fanatics pull weapons from behind their backs like they are drawing swords. Their weapons of choice: goddess statues the length of their arms. The divinity overflowing from the sculptures of the simply attired woman makes them look like goddess statues from any angle.

"I will take you on if you want to fight." Iris rummages through a wooden chest in the corner. Just when I'm wondering what she's going to procure, it turns out to be another goddess statue.

If I ever meet Goddess Sadia, I think I'll tell her that there are people in this world brawling with her statues.

Both parties are facing off, prepared to go at it statue to statue. Now's as good a time as ever to make a run for it. Pressed up against the wall, I gradually advance toward the exit, but then stop halfway. I can't just leave them here to kill each other with goddess statues.

## Another World's Zombie Apocalypse Is Not My Problem!

"Ahem... Why don't you all stop this nonsense? Okay? Why don't we peacefully talk things out—"

"We have nothing to say to this bitch!"

"I don't want to speak with these bastards either! My ears will rot off!"

Instead of calming down, they've become more argumentative. It's no use. They show no signs of stopping.

The floorboards creak, signaling both sides to commence the fight—but before they can clash statues, thundering footsteps can be heard pounding the ground, accompanied by crashing and clanging.

Five knights storm the room from the broken door. Without hesitating, they take down the fanatics, restraining them in the blink of an eye.

"Lady Mizuha!"

"Lex!"

Lex is among the knights.

"...I am very glad to see you safe and well, m'lady."

"Thanks. I knew you'd come for me." Though I didn't think he would come this soon. "How did you know I was here?"

"We tracked the fanatics to this place. They began acting suspiciously after you disappeared, which led us to believe it was somehow related."

So they were able to show up here because of their observation of the fanatics' actions. This is one thing I should be grateful to the fanatics for.

"This is the holy headquarters of the Church of Our Lady Mizuha. Everyone, even Royal Knights, must leave if they are not believers."

"Then I needn't leave, for I am a member of the Church of Our Lady Mizuha."

"Uh? Lex? What random things are you claiming this time?"

"Y-You are my brother in the faith...?"

Oh my gosh. Iris even believes him.

Lex seals the deal with a daring smile. "I have been worshipping her since long before you."

"A more mature brother in the faith...?" Iris jerks her head back as if she's been struck by a shocking blow. A fraction of a second later, she's giving her head a hard shake. "Y-You nearly had me fooled...! You are the heathen trying to steal Goddess Mizuha from Iris! That is, the enemy!"

Iris charges at Lex with the goddess statue. But Lex immediately seizes her wrists, curtailing her movement. Not even Iris and her superhuman strength are a match for Lex, who fights for a living.

"Quietly surrender… The crime of abducting Lady Mizuha, the savior of our kingdom, is a heavy one." Shortly after that, Iris and the fanatics are bound in rope, their next destination: the dungeons. "This way, Lady Mizuha. Let us be on our way."

"O-Okay…" With Lex leading the way, I try to leave the room.

"Give her back! Give Iris's goddess baaaaaaaack!" Iris has begun violently struggling with such force the rope cuts into her bound hands and feet. Her skin bloodied from the ropes is too much to look at.

"Lex, give me a moment with her." I return to where Iris is detained and crouch down until my gaze is level with hers. "Iris, you should know, I am not really the Goddess."

"Liar! Goddess Mizuha is the Goddess!"

"You won't believe me?"

"The Goddess is all Iris has! The Goddess will light up my world!"

Her crazed shouts help me remember she was raised in an orphanage.

People who grew up in orphanages aren't the only ones who feel disappointed in the world. It's probably presumptuous and wrong of me to pity her, but even so, the feeling that I shouldn't just abandon her here is stronger than anything else. More than that, while Iris is physically older than me, she's mentally closer to a child.

"Lex, is it possible you could free her?"

"That is a difficult request… First of all, you will be put in harm's way again, Lady Mizuha."

"It'll probably be okay." I return my gaze to Iris's eyes and softly try to persuade her. "Say, Iris, do you want to be tossed in the dungeon?"

"No, I don't. I won't be able to see my goddess again…"

"Then are you willing to promise never to hurt another person again?"

"Can I start the Church of Our Lady Mizuha?"

"No. You must promise not to do that either."

"Booooooooo…" Iris continues moaning in mental anguish.

Ten seconds after I stifle my desire to make a joke about just how bad she wants to open a church in my name, she nods her head with

## Another World's Zombie Apocalypse Is Not My Problem!

pursed lips.

"I...promise."

"Good girl, good girl." As a reward, I pat her on the head in the same way she enjoyed earlier. Iris's facial muscles slacken into a blissful smile. Her inherent qualities are good, but she can also be extremely cute. Anyone would take to her if she was always like this. What a shame.

"W-We will listen to anything you say, so please give us any punishment other than the zombie dungeons!" The fanatics start begging after Iris's ropes are untied.

"Lex, go ahead and free them too."

"B-But—"

"It's not fair if Iris is the only one let off the hook."

"...As you command, m'lady." Lex reluctantly orders the other knights with a look to undo the ropes.

The freed fanatics regain their smiles. I hate to ruin their moment of happiness, but they must be warned with as much intimidation as I can muster.

"I won't stop Lex and the knights from punishing you the next time you hurt someone. Also, you shouldn't defile the goddess statues like that. You'll only sadden her by doing such things."

"But then how can we deliver divine punishment...?"

"It isn't supposed to come from you guys, is it?"

"We are Goddess Sadia's representatives on this land and—"

"You are forbidden from dishing out divine punishment. You swore to listen to anything I say."

"W-We shall do as you command."

"Good. As long as you understand," I answer with a satisfied smile. I'm glad things ended peacefully. That sums up my feelings on the whole thing.

"Oi, Iris. It seems like you were right all along," the fanatic leader concedes.

"There is no greater joy for me than you seeing the light. I leave the rest in your hands."

"You can count on us...!"

Iris and the fanatic leader are exchanging a firm handshake over something or other. I'm not really sure what just happened, but I guess this is case closed with their reconciliation...right?

**Haru Yayari**

◆Chapter 18: Handshake Sessions and Ardent Fans

**THINGS** started going amiss after I finished purifying the outlying regions and returned to the capital with Lex.

"Zombies! Zombies in the city!" someone screams.

"No way! I thought we got rid of the city dwellers?!" I can't believe my ears.

"Some may have slipped in overnight without our notice," Lex frets.

"But they can't get in except through the gates or over the walls. How could we miss that?"

"Zombies over here too!" comes a scream from another location.

"R-Run!"

The confusion proliferates, sending people running for their lives. Did several dozen zombies break in? Or has the infection found a new way of spreading? Whatever the case is—

"We don't have time to sit and chat about it…"

"Indeed. For now, we should hurry to where the zombies are running amok!"

"**HUMANS** have reverted into zombies?"

After handling the zombies that had suddenly popped up in the capital, Lex and I headed straight to where Pino was working in the Royal Library.

## Another World's Zombie Apocalypse Is Not My Problem!

"Yeah. The witnesses all gave the same testimony, so it can't be wrong. I took care of it on the spot since there weren't too many and it's daytime, but—"

"The people are disturbed by the discovery that some are turning back into zombies, right?" Pino concludes from where he's sitting, reading a hefty book.

"A significant number of citizens observed it happen, so I want to put an end to the chaos fast," Lex continues, uncaring that he's interrupting Pino's book time.

"And that is why you came to me?" Pino sighs while shutting his book and shoots me a nasty look. "I'm very busy, though. Aren't I, Miss Priestess?"

"I am beyond grateful and can never be grateful enough for what you are doing, Pino. Yes, indeedy."

We're adding this incident on top of his assisting me in finding a way home. I can't argue with him.

"Well, it's fine this time," Pino relents, changing moods. "It could be caused by the addition of a new external factor, but… First, what information do you have on the rezombified people?"

"Everything we know is included in this report."

Pino accepts the report from Lex and scans it. "Interesting. A lot of knights. And many of them members of the Royal Knights…" he mutters, suspiciously looking Lex over.

"Wh-What is it?"

"Nothing. By the way, Miss Priestess, is Her Highness in good health?" Pino swings his gaze from Lex to me.

"Yeah, she's doing well. Why?"

"I see. So that's what this is."

"Did you figure something out?"

Pino nods confidently. "Zombie purification is very likely not a permanent solution. The effects weaken over time since they last touched you, eventually ending in them reverting to zombies. The reason there's a high number of Royal Knights among the rezombified is that they were the first to be purified."

I had saved the capital city full of normal citizens for last, starting my purification process with the knight-filled castle. Pino's not mistaken in what he's saying—except for one thing.

"Then why is Cia unaffected? I returned her to human long before the others."

"Simple—because she's often in physical contact with you."

We wash each other's backs during our baths, sleep together, and even hold hands often. There's no question I touch her more than anyone else.

"Does that mean their time as humans can be extended by touching me?"

"That is what it means, yes."

"Ugh. Then I have to touch everyone constantly for the rest of my life? I'm not big on that idea…"

"According to my conjecture, if you repeat the process several times, the curse will diminish, and you won't need to purify that person again."

"I sure hope so, or else I'll go insane."

Girls and women are one thing, but I don't want to keep touching strange men I don't know. I've been doing it only because it's necessary to purify them; it's not like I'm perfectly fine with it.

"If that is the case, we must remedy the matter with urgency. How should we proceed?" Lex asks.

"It needs to be an efficient method that lets me touch a lot of people at once," I say, murmuring "Hmm" along with Lex.

"I have an idea," Pino says, smirking. "Let's hold a handshake session."

A tent is temporarily set up near the outer castle gate. The handshake session is going to be held there.

"We need to test and see first."

At Pino's advice, five hundred people have been gathered for the first session. This is fewer people than I purified on my first day making the rounds in the city, though seeing them all lined up like this makes it feel like there are even more. Thanks to the hardworking knights, people are waiting in an orderly line, but I shudder at the thought of them suddenly rushing at me in confusion.

"Please shake Priestess Mizuha's hand in order! Please be quick because there is a line behind you! Please don't push!" Lex shouts

## Another World's Zombie Apocalypse Is Not My Problem!

through his hands cupped like a megaphone. He isn't acting like I'd expect a knight to in this situation. He's more like a security guard cosplaying as a knight.

In any case, the handshake session has begun. Men and women of all ages have come. I spend less than ten seconds with each person, but they all leave different impressions.

"Thanks, Holy Priestess!"

"I am truly...truly grateful to you."

Most people express their gratitude. I struggle with how to react to those among them who rub their hands together, prayerfully exclaiming, "Goddess be thanked! Goddess praise you!"

The knights did the most work bringing these people back, but I also worked hard every day to the point of dizziness. I can greet them with a genuine smile when I think their presence here is the result of what we did.

"Th-This girl's saliva is... GULP!"

"I shall never wash the hand you touched, Priestess!"

"Haaah...haaah...haah..."

My smile accidentally slips a little—no, a lot—whenever the occasional heavy-breathing pervert slips into the line. Forcing my twitching lips up, I somehow manage to shake their hands.

"Hey, Lex? I've been thinking about this for a while now, but aren't there one too many weirdos in Grantz?"

"That just goes to show how happy everyone is to shake your hand, Lady Mizuha."

I believe there is a limit to what's appropriate behavior when someone is excited! Still, though, I never thought the day would come in my life when I would be holding a handshake session.

For starters, I'm not all sparkly and cheery like an idol, and aside from a small group of perverts, the people coming to shake my hand are here with the wholehearted desire not to turn back into zombies. It's still an unexpected development for me, though.

"Lady Mizuha, are you fatigued?"

"A little, yeah. But it doesn't seem to tire me out as much as when I turn zombies back into humans. You can slightly increase the number of people starting tomorrow."

Having said that, I'm burning out from shaking hands with more

## Haru Yayari

people than I had expected. It wouldn't be right to greet them with a sour face, so I'm smiling and sitting up straight mostly because I don't want them to see me slouching. I can't ever put my arm down either. This is more tiring than anything else.

But it's better than everyone turning back into zombies and having to go through that again, so I'll push through it. Mentally encouraging myself, I lift my head and see someone familiar standing in front of me.

"Excuse me, weren't you here earlier…?" I ask.

"You remembered me, MIZUHA!"

On top of his being first in line, he squeezed my hand for an awfully long time, so I remember him well from the horrible impression he left.

"Uggh," I quietly whimper. Spotting my obviously uncomfortable expression, Lex deals with him in my place.

"My apologies, sir, but each person gets only one handshake."

"Lex Irvine… You dare stand in my way?"

"Lord Rowadan. Even you are expected to follow the rules. Will one of you men escort Lord Rowadan away?"

A knight runs over and ushers the man out of line. "Dirty scoundrel! Unhand me!" The man struggles but is powerless against a knight. He's dragged away until he's out of sight.

After the commotion is over, I ask Lex about it. "Do you know that man?"

"Lord Keith Rowadan. He is the son of the seigneur of Lajina Seigneury located to the southwest of the capital."

"You mean he's a nobleman?"

"That would make him one, yes."

"Heh," I utter, indifferent. Between his mushroom-cut red hair and fancy crimson vest, he had the exaggerated look of a nobleman, but he was so desperate, he came off as a totally inconsequential person.

…*Well, it's not like I'll see him again, so it's not my problem,* I think, but boy am I mistaken.

"Hi there. I've come to see you again, MiZUha!" Keith shows up a short while later looking all nonchalant and innocent.

Seeing his sunny smile, I dispassionately say, "Lex."

"As you command, m'lady." At Lex's orders, two knights seize Keith's arms and begin dragging him away.

"P-Please wait! I fell in love with you at first sight!"

## Another World's Zombie Apocalypse Is Not My Problem!

"Ueehh?" I croak in a weird voice. His confession appears to send shockwaves through the crowd. I'm not the one who confessed my love in front of them, yet I'm drowning in embarrassment.

"How is that for a reason?!"

"Unfortunately, that is not a valid reason."

Keith is hauled farther away by the knights at Lex's ruthless judgment. But he hasn't given up yet, it seems.

"Damn it! You leave me no choice but to become a zombie to see you again!"

"You will only tire me out, so seriously, drop the idea." His extremely idiotic plan sweeps away my embarrassment. Annoyed, I put a question to him. "Why are you so obsessed with me? I believe today is the first time we've spoken…"

"But we met long before today! Indeed, it was on that day you saved me from being a zombie…" He takes an exaggerated pose like he's acting out a reminiscing scene in a play. "You were shining when I saw you!"

"That would be the purification light."

"My heart was pounding so hard my chest hurt!"

"Sorry about that. I probably punched you in the chest…"

"And I'm okay with that!"

What happened to his heart-pounding moment?

"I'm sorry. I can't reciprocate your feelings."

"Why don't you understand how I feel for you…?!"

"No, I am rejecting your feelings because I do understand." No matter how much I reject him, Keith won't give up.

"You can play and live in luxury for the rest of your life if you become my wife. You can do whatever you want with the vast lands of Lajina!"

"Lord Rowadan, that region is still infected by the zombie blight."

"……"

This guy is a mess. I'm starting to pity him a smidge. Not that I'm going to accept his affections because of it, though.

"I see the truth now! This man is the reason why." Keith, having arrived at what's likely the wrong conclusion, throws off the knights and thrusts his finger at Lex. "Lex Irvine! Duel me right here and now!"

"What would you like me to do, m'lady?" Lex asks me with a troubled look.

"Hmm, he seems like the type to throw another fit if you refuse."

"In that case, I shall quickly teach him a lesson."

A typical tragic heroine would probably cry, "Please don't fight over me!" Too bad I'm no damsel in distress—I don't remember ever promising myself to the winner. They're welcome to go at it all they want.

"Try not to put him in the hospital, though," I say, voicing my one concern. "I can heal him with my left hand, but I'd rather not."

"You can set your fears at ease on that front."

I wouldn't expect anything less of Grantz Kingdom's number-one swordsman. He's full of confidence.

And so, the sudden duel commences. They charge at each other with wooden swords, but it's over in an instant, ending with Lex's overwhelming victory. Without even swinging his sword, Keith is knocked to the ground a second after they start.

"Why?! Why has God bestowed this trial upon me?!" Keith pounds his annoyance out on the ground. What in the world is he fighting? "I'll never give up! I will absolutely get you—"

"Boss Lady! Boss Man!" Rosso's shout cuts through the noise as he pushes his way through the crowd to us.

"Rosso? What's wrong?"

"Nothin'! I came because I heard you're doing some sorta handshake thingy. Oh, here are some refreshments!" Oblivious to the tense mood, Rosso hands me the paper bag he was holding with both hands. A savory scent spills from the bag.

Could this be what I think it is? Full of hope, I check what's inside. "I knew it!" I exclaim. "It's bread!"

"You remember the wheat rations the knights distributed the other day? My kid sister baked bread with it."

"Can I eat it?"

"Go right ahead. Though she said it doesn't have much taste because she hurried with grinding the wheat into flour."

I pull out what looks like a bread roll and take a bite. I was prepared for the lack of sweetness because of the difficulty involved in obtaining sugar and butter, but frankly, the hard, stiff texture makes it not taste very good. Still, since it's a gift, I force a smile.

## Another World's Zombie Apocalypse Is Not My Problem!

"You don't hafta pretend," Rosso informs me with an understanding grin. "My kid sister was prepared for it to taste bad this time."

"...Sorry."

"She's gonna keep attempting it until she gets it right, so please try it again when she does."

"I'd absolutely love to!" I enthusiastically exclaim, then suddenly remember the situation. We are still the center of attention. Rosso finally notices the unusual state of things.

"Somethin' go down 'round here?"

"Yeah, a couple of things."

It'd take too long to— Actually, it wouldn't take that long to explain. A nobleman is persistently trying to court me—that about sums it up. I just don't feel comfortable explaining it like that in front of the guy.

Meanwhile, said guy is trembling as he shakes his head. "Boss Lady... Boss Man... Could it be? Are they already a thing...? It can't be true..." Keith's face twists. "NOOOOOOOOOOOOOOOOO!" He finally runs off, wailing. The crowd moves away from him so fast, it's obvious they don't want to be involved in his affairs.

"He left."

"What's that guy's problem?" Rosso watches Keith fleeing like he's observing a bizarre spectacle.

Lex stands beside me. "Mayhap he misconstrued me and Lady Mizuha as husband and wife?"

"He probably did."

Considering he challenged Lex to a duel, the chances of that are high.

"Pardon the foolish question, Lady Mizuha, but is it all right for you to not go and set the story straight?"

"Hmm... I'd rather leave it this way since he's less likely to stalk me."

"I see. Is that how it works?" Lex sounds convinced. His face doesn't show even a hint of a reaction. Does he think nothing of others believing we're married? Or does he accept it simply as a part of his job? Whatever the reason, I wish he would be a little shaken up by it.

"Oh? Is something the matter, Lady Mizuha?"

"Nope. Nothing." I avert my eyes from him before furtively stealing a side-glance.

Well, I'd take Lex any day over that spoiled nobleman.

## ◆Chapter 19: Separation and Reunion

"**WHAT** do you think he wants to talk about?"

I'm walking side by side through the castle corridors with Lex. About an hour ago, when I returned to the city after finishing up my daily purification of the outlying regions, Sir Oden summoned us, saying, "I have something to discuss with you both. Please come to the castle once you're finished."

"Mayhap it has something to do with procuring raw materials. We are burning through wood faster than we feared," Lex explains.

"But is that enough of a reason to call us all the way back to the castle, and into the royal audience chamber at that? Couldn't he have just put in his request when he saw us? Why this out-of-the-ordinary change?"

"Y-You make a valid point..."

Talking the whole way there, we arrive at the audience chamber. I've visited it on countless occasions since I started living in the castle, but I'm always stunned by its sheer size. Although traces of damage can be seen here and there from its time under zombie rule, you can still feel the majestic and solemn atmosphere it was built to inspire.

"I have been waiting for you, Big Sister." Cia stands from the innermost throne and welcomes me.

Since we normally don't stand on formality when we speak, this is a curious spectacle for me. But with no one aside from Sir Oden around, there's no need for me to be unduly nervous.

Lex suddenly kneels on one knee and lowers his head. There's

### Another World's Zombie Apocalypse Is Not My Problem!

nothing strange about that when he's before his princess and within the formal setting of the audience chamber.

"Should I bow too?"

"No. Please stay as you are. Lex, please be at ease too."

"Yes, Your Highness," Lex replies shortly, rising.

Once he's on his feet again, I make my inquiry known. "Can we get down to business now? Why did you call us here today?"

"Allow me to explain," Sir Oden answers, stepping forward from his spot just behind the throne. "We have two matters to discuss. First, we would like to request your assistance in resupplying the overwhelming shortage of lumber."

"Then the shortage has indeed become a problem, as we predicted," Lex remarks.

"Veritably. Structures built with stone are still intact, but anything that used wood has faced severe erosion. Most wooden structures are in a state of needing to be rebuilt from the ground up. Lady Mizuha, I apologize for relying on you for everything, but…will you assist in this matter?"

"Of course."

Spitting on things still doesn't sit well with me, but it does no harm aside from the fatigue it causes me. I have no reason to refuse when it leads to a safer place for me to eat and sleep.

"You have my gratitude."

"Please accept my heartfelt gratitude as well," Cia says, expressing her thanks after Sir Oden. Being thanked is more uncomfortable for me than anything else.

"Uh… Please don't feel bad. You aren't asking too much of me. Anyway! You said there are two matters. What is the second?"

"Very well. I shall speak of it next." Sir Oden is about to tell me when Cia speaks over him.

"Captain Oden. I am against this—"

"Your Highness, this is necessary."

"…If you say so," Cia weakly concedes. Our eyes meet, but she quickly looks away.

I'm briefly worried that she's come to hate me, but that doesn't seem to be the case. Not only is she gnawing on her lower lip, but she's curled her hands into tight fists in her lap.

Whether he knows how she feels or not, Sir Oden cuts to the chase in a commanding voice. "Though the process has been slow, the kingdom has gradually regained a state of calm. The senate has decided to restructure the Royal Knights back to their former positions in order to speed along the restoration."

"So that is what this is about…" Lex seems to have figured it out, but I still have no clue. Stuck as the only confused party, I watch as Sir Oden faces Lex with the most rigid, demanding expression yet.

"Lex Irvine, you are hereby relieved of your duties as the holy priestess's guard. From henceforth, you are to serve as Her Highness the Princess's knight."

**THE** following morning, I'm waiting in front of the outer castle gate when two knights come before me.

"If I'm not mistaken, we've met before…" I venture.

"We are honored to be in your presence again."

They are the two knights who volunteered to be bait when we were trying to take back the castle from the super-active night zombies. I'm not necessarily on familiar terms with them, but I'm relieved from the bottom of my heart that I was assigned people I know.

"I'm sorry you had to be reassigned as my guards."

"Please don't be sorry!"

"We applied for this assignment."

They applied for it?

"Why?" I ask, earning a few blank blinks from them.

"Because of that, of course…yeah?"

"Y-Yeah."

What are they talking about? It doesn't help that they both have goofy grins. I feel bad saying this about people who volunteered to protect me, but they creep me out. Noticing my eyes have narrowed in on them, they quickly straighten up.

"We haven't introduced ourselves yet. I am Kurt Becker."

"Julian Graz."

Sir Kurt is a charming young man with short hair, while Sir Julian is a good-looking young man with long hair who gives off the impression

**Another World's Zombie Apocalypse Is Not My Problem!**

of someone who's a bit of a stiff. As I'm thinking about how their names sound German, both men tap their fists to their chests in salute.

"I may be inadequate to fill in Sir Lex's boots, but...I will do my very best as your guard, Lady Mizuha," Sir Kurt swears, his expression staunch.

Lex has been by my side since the day I arrived in this world. That's why his being removed from my guard detail didn't feel real to me, but...the reality has finally set in.

I slowly tip my head. "I will be counting on you both."

**AFTER** joining up with the Raw Materials Harvesting and Transportation Squad, we depart for the forest. Meadows and grasslands abound in the nearby areas I had purified in the days prior. Thanks to that, I feel revitalized by inhaling deeply of the fresh, clean air, free of zombie stank.

"Excuse me... Has Lex always been Cia's personal guard?" I ask Sir Kurt along the way.

"Yes, milady," he answers, keeping pace with me. "You know of the Royal Knights, yes?"

"First, you have ordinary soldiers, then the Order of the Knights, and only a select few of those knights can become Royal Knights, right?" I confirm, repeating what Lex had told me before.

"Only the best of the best knights can become Royal Knights, to be precise. And it is only the strongest of the Royal Knights who can serve as personal guards to royalty."

"Then what about Sir Oden?"

I've seen Lex in action enough times to know he's strong. Judging from his charge attacks alone, Sir Oden isn't lacking in the strength department either.

"Captain Oden's duties as captain of the knights take precedence."

"Then Lex isn't necessarily stronger than Sir Oden," I assume.

"That's open to debate," Sir Julian interjects, joining our conversation. "He is normally not all there, but"—so I'm not the only one who thinks he has a few screws loose— "I would say Lex is the far superior swordsman."

His normal behavior being what it is, it's never really stuck with me that Lex is a strong fighter, but they make it sound like he's much more amazing than I give him credit for. I'm starting to regret after the fact that I used and abused him a little too much.

And so, we continue walking for another thirty minutes or thereabouts, chatting about nonessential stuff until we arrive at our destination.

"This is the Great Oak Forest. Plenty of fine trees excellent for use as building materials grow here, but…"

"The zombie rot hit this place hard, huh?"

All the large trees growing amid swaths of venomous purple grass are peeling, crumbling, molting, and splitting down the middle, creating a lurid forest. Buildings using these trees as material will surely crumble.

"Looks like it's my turn now. Excuse me! Will you all please turn the other way?" I address the soldiers in the squad.

"I would love to witness the act of purification if you would so allow—"

"Please turn around." I flash a murderous smile, causing everyone to flinch and whirl around until their backs are to me. I inwardly sigh. Being around people I'm not comfortable with is tiring. Lex made my life a lot easier on that front. Wait, what am I thinking?

Shaking my head, I quickly spit on the ground. Purification spreads to the trees. Bark regrows on the peeling trunks, followed shortly by the rest of the tree flourishing until green leaves sprout from all the branches. Before long, greenery fills the forest, drawing sighs of awe from the soldiers and knights.

I spin around and entrust the rest to them. "I'm finished. Please take care of the rest."

The soldiers set about harvesting trees, chopping them down left and right before piling them on the carts. Taking into account that the forest might rot again once we leave, the soldiers plan to take every tree they fell with them. We have a shortage of helping hands and few carts capable of transporting full-grown trees. It doesn't take long before the soldiers have all the carts fully loaded.

"Phew…" I sit on a downed log and take a break. Most of the work is finished, aside from tying down the lumber to keep it from rolling out of the carts.

## Another World's Zombie Apocalypse Is Not My Problem!

"We finished up much faster than I had expected," Sir Kurt comments, taking up position at my side. "This, too, was only possible with your assistance, Lady Mizuha."

"I've barely done anything, though. Ahaha," I say with a dry laugh. The trees are far too heavy for me to carry, so I'd just get in their way if I tried. In the end, I could only watch the soldiers do all the work.

"Didn't you fetch water for us?"

"Only because I had nothing better to do."

I had discovered a low cliff a short walk from here. I purified the small lake that happened to be at the bottom of the cliff and made several round trips carrying buckets of water from there to where the men were working.

"The men were grateful for your thoughtfulness."

"It was more me trying to find a job to do, but I'm glad it was appreciated."

"OINK!" A pig's snort interrupts our casual conversation. I sweep my gaze over the surrounding woods until I spot a pig several feet away. It looks exactly like the pigs in my world. Our eyes meet for a second before the pig quickly turns its rump toward me and trots away.

Why is there a lone pig here? I'm trying to figure it out, when all of a sudden my whole body shudders. Seconds later, I hear trees snapping and breaking. I've got a seriously bad feeling about this. Trees fall over in the direction the pig disappeared in, revealing an enormous human-shaped zombie.

"Boneless Ham…!"

Boneless Ham's roar echoes through the forest. Shock courses through the soldiers. Not only have some fallen to their knees, but others flee in different directions. And they call themselves soldiers?!

"Please calm down, everyone! It's still light out! He probably can't r—"

He can't run—that's what I was about to say, when Boneless Ham breaks into a sprint, his heavy feet pounding the ground.

"H-He can freakin' run?!"

I'd assumed Boneless Ham couldn't move fast in daylight, like the other zombies, but my assumptions were wrong! The soldiers I had just started to get under control fall into an even worse panic. They scatter every which way.

"Please run away too, Lady Mizuha!" Sir Kurt bravely steps in front of Boneless Ham's path and throws rocks at it. Then he spins around and bolts in the opposite direction of everyone else. "Come here, fatso! I'll take you on!"

Sir Kurt is trying to lure it away as bait, but Boneless Ham doesn't even look his way as it fixates its charge on me.

"No way?! Why is it coming straight for me?!"

I whirl around and flee. Boneless Ham is so heavy, the ground shakes with its every footstep. I glance over my shoulder and see Boneless Ham smashing down trees and plowing through soldiers as it bears down on me.

I can purify him if I can just touch him somehow, but with his charging me like this, I'll sooner turn into a Mizuha pancake than be able to get my right hand on him. I'm done for the moment he gets close. If I'm not squashed under him, I'll be splattered all over by his hammer-like arms. On the bright side, he's significantly slower than the regular zombies during their souped-up night mode. I'm just barely keeping ahead of it because of that. The question is: Just how long can I keep this up?

"Lady Mizuha!"

"Sir Julian! That THING is clearly after me! You'd better get away from me!" I shout in warning to Sir Julian, who's running parallel to me. Instead of distancing himself, he runs closer. He glances once at Boneless Ham before returning his gaze to me.

"Draw him to the place where you purified the water!" he instructs.

"Good idea! I'll try to get him to fall in there!"

Zombies are weakened by purified water. Our last battle with a Boneless Ham proved they have the same weakness. I'll just keep running until I can dive off the cliff into the water, bringing the Boneless Ham down with me!

"Lady Mizuha!"

"Wha-?!"

Shoved from behind, I tumble on the ground. Confused about what just happened, I narrowly catch sight of a large tree crashing into Sir Julian. Boneless Ham must have thrown it! Sir Julian falls end over end, bouncing several times off the ground until he stops moving altogether.

"Sir Julian!"

## Another World's Zombie Apocalypse Is Not My Problem!

"I am…alive…m-milady," he splutters between gasps for air. "Please! Run away!"

Blood is spurting from his head, and he can barely move. He's seriously injured. I can heal him with my left hand—

Boneless Ham's ferocious roar immediately dissuades me. It's almost here. This freakazoid of a zombie is after me. One wrong move and I could get Sir Julian killed in the process.

Mind made up, I kick off with my right leg to run, but a painful sting in my ankle turns my run into more of a fast limp. I might have sprained it when I tried to catch my balance after he shoved me. Understanding why I'm hurt doesn't do anything to help me move faster, though. Boneless Ham is charging right at me from the closest distance yet.

I'm done for.

A horse's neigh echoes through the forest like a beacon of hope.

"Take my hand!" a familiar voice commands.

## Another World's Zombie Apocalypse Is Not My Problem!

For a moment, my brain doesn't process in the confusion, but I reach out for that hand faster than I put the pieces together. My body is yanked into the air. As soon as I am on the horse's—Vianta's—back, I shout to the knight gripping the reins behind me.

"Lex...why are you—?!" *Here; I thought you were supposed to be on Cia's guard detail*—is what I'm about to ask when he speaks over me.

"Save your questions for after we take that monstrosity down!"

Boneless Ham remains in hot pursuit even after I'm escaping by horse. I have loads of questions for Lex, but I have to get my head in the game first so I can live to hear the answer!

"There's a small lake up ahead! We just have to drop him in it!"

"Will do, m'lady!"

Traveling by horse gets us to our destination in no time. I can't see the lake, but I do see where the ground falls off. The lake is below.

"Please hold on tight, m'lady!"

"What?! You aren't about to—"

"We are going to jump it!"

Vianta picks up speed and leaps off the cliff. A blue sky fills my vision that had nothing but trees and leaves in it until now. Just how high did Vianta jump?! After what seemed like being suspended in midair for a long time, the shock of impact courses from my butt up through my body.

Rather than feel relieved we've safely landed, I'm more surprised we leaped over the entire lake. Small though it is, it should've been impossible for a person—or even a horse—to jump over. Apparently, the horses of this world are capable of things not possible for horses in my world.

Three whole beats after we land, Boneless Ham charges onto the top of the cliff. Just when I thought it'd careen right off the ledge and into the lake, it skids to a halt at the last second. The sheer weight of it, though, works against it as the ground beneath its feet crumbles. It loses balance, the top half of its body swaying to stay upright.

"Fall on down, monster!"

Swinging its large arms through the air, it manages to hold its ground. Is it my imagination, or did Boneless Ham's grotesquely big mouth twist up in a triumphant sneer? We almost had it too!

"URAAAAAAAAAAH!"

Just as I hear that abrupt battle cry, Boneless Ham's massive body pitches forward. Unable to catch itself this time, it falls into the lake! KER-SPLASH! Water sprays everywhere in a giant tidal wave. The area is soaked by droplets as if a sudden spring rain had fallen.

"Looks like I somehow managed to steal the show."

"Sir Kurt!"

Sir Kurt is holding up a shield on top of the cliff. He literally had perfect timing! I shift my gaze from Sir Kurt down to the lake where Boneless Ham is lifelessly floating at the surface. Purification will be a piece of cake now.

**SIR** Julian fully recovered from his wounds with a touch from my left hand. It drained the energy completely out of me, leaving me exhausted, but I'd take that any day over letting him die. With the chaos under control, the soldiers are preparing for the journey home.

"Okay…time for you to spill. Why did you come here? Or rather, how were you allowed to come?" I ask Lex, who is standing at my side watching the soldiers put things in order.

"I was relieved of my duty as royal guard."

"You were? Why?"

"I was there in body, but not in spirit. That mind-set seems to have been the reason."

"Do you mean…"

What do I do if I get this wrong? With that fear in the back of my mind, I can think of only one reason why he wouldn't be there in spirit. Seeing Lex's awkward smile gives me confidence that I have the right idea.

Lex takes on a serious expression and slowly goes down on one knee. "If it so pleases you, please make me, Lex Irvine, your knight, Lady Mizuha."

I can't help blinking at this unexpected turn of events. Honestly, a part of me rejoiced when I heard he was relieved from his duties as Cia's guard. Sir Kurt and Sir Julian are very good men, too, but somehow it just didn't seem the same with them.

That's why I'm delighted Lex has returned to my side again like this.

## Another World's Zombie Apocalypse Is Not My Problem!

I'm genuinely happy to hear he wants to serve me. But...while I don't know much about knights, I get the sense this isn't something I should accept with half-hearted feelings.

"Lex, there is something I want you to know."

"...Yes, m'lady?"

"Do you remember...when I told you how I came from another world?"

"Yes, around the time we first met."

At the time, I wasn't sure if Lex believed me or not from his response, "It only affirms you are our holy priestess."

"Yeah, that's the one. It's the truth. So you see, Pino is searching for a way for me to return to that world. That's why—"

—I might disappear from this world forever. Lex speaks sooner than I can tell him that, though. "In that case, I shall become your sword and shield for the duration of your time in this world, Lady Mizuha."

His declaration, without an ounce of hesitation, leaves me blinking in disbelief. And then, I giggle behind my hand. "Weirdo. You almost sound like a real knight, Lex."

"I am a real knight." Lex raises his head, another joyous smile gracing his handsome visage.

"I'm also...comfortable with you. Other people stress me out."

"Pardon the question, but is that something for me to be happy about?"

"I'll leave that to your imagination." I flash a teasing grin. I can see the expedition squad has finished preparations for the journey home; they seem to be waiting for us now. "Ready to go home?" On my way to join the others, I abruptly turn around and call his name. "Lex! I'm looking forward to our continued time together!"

"...Me too, m'lady!"

Haru Yayari

◆Chapter 20: The Number-One Person I Don't Want to See on a Day Off

**SEVERAL** days after going on the expedition to harvest resources, I've received a day off from my purification duties. I didn't want a break—Cia asked me to take the time off. She seems to think I've been working too much. I feel guilty resting when everyone else is working hard toward restoration, but…the truth of the matter is that my body is aching and cracking all over from walking so much, so I gladly took her up on the offer.

That being said, I didn't have anything in particular I wanted to do with this free time. Wide-scale revitalization of the capital has only recently been undertaken, and they haven't gotten around to fixing up the entertainment venues. In the end, I woke up and left the castle like usual, and I've been spending my time since walking down the capital's main street with Lex.

"This has kind of become our routine, huh?"

"You mean…walking around the capital?"

"Yep. Well, I don't dislike doing it, so it's fine by me. It's kind of a relief to see the city gradually rebuild too."

The cityscape changes with every visit. Walls that were missing stones and crumbling yesterday are standing tall and strong today. Structures are erected on formerly vacant lots. And it's not just the buildings or the physical objects: as the number of people increases, so does the number of smiles. I don't know what this city looked like originally. Maybe being here isn't all that uncomfortable for me anymore because it feels like I am growing with the city.

"I wish you could see Grantz Kingdom in all its glory, Lady Mizuha," Lex says sadly.

"...Lex."

He almost makes it sound like I'll never see the completely restored Grantz. I understand what he means by that. Even I want to see things through to the end. But—

"Miss!"

I turn toward the familiar voice and find a face I know there. It's the first boy I healed. He's running up to me.

"This is my thanks for last time!" He holds out the bouquet he was hiding behind his back. Quietly swaying in his hand are flowers with four large petals the same bright red as roses.

"Wow! Those are beautiful!" I exclaim.

"They were growing near my house!"

"Thank you!"

"Ehehe! I'd better get going now. Mommy will yell at me if I'm late."

"Okay! See you next time!" I'm quietly watching the boy leave when Lex steps next to me.

"Good to see him doing well."

"Yeah... Purification is definitely useful, but the power to heal is really handy."

Using either one drains the life out of me, but I can regain my energy by eating and sleeping. That's hardly a price to pay.

"And that is precisely why this holy power made its home in one with a pure and true heart—you, Lady Mizuha."

"You think too highly of me. Even I might abuse these powers, you know?"

"I shall accompany you if you do."

"Oh gosh, that'd make it hard to do anything bad..."

"It is that side of you, m'lady." Lex laughs at me.

It's one thing for me to walk the dark path, but I'd have reservations about making someone my accomplice in it. Obviously, I don't plan to do anything evil with my powers, but I feel like I couldn't even on the off chance I wanted to.

"Sorry about today," I apologize. "You could have taken it easy if I had rested."

"Thank you for being thoughtful of me. However, you can rest assured that I am barely fatigued."

He isn't putting up a front; this is how he really feels. Lex is full of life.

"Whenever I see you like that, it really makes you seem like a knight."

"I train on a daily basis, after all."

"I'm pretty confident in my stamina, though."

"You certainly are more active, or rather, more energetic than other women, Lady Mizuha."

"Oh, I'm sure I'm far from being a lady. Hmph." I grumpily point my chin the other way.

Flustered, Lex circles around until he's facing me. "N-Not at all, m'lady! I swear I did not mean it in that way! I believe it is one of your charms and— L-Lady Mizuha?"

Darn. He saw me trying to restrain my laughter. Now that the cat's out of the bag, I stick my tongue out at him. "Sorry, I was teasing you."

"Th-That is not very nice…" Lex places his hand on his chest like he's thoroughly relieved it was a joke. I wasn't randomly teasing him for nothing, though.

"That's payback for you suddenly showing up the other day."

"Y-You don't leave me much room for rebuttal when you bring that up…"

"Don't get me wrong. I'm grateful you saved me. But this and that are different, okay?"

I wanted to get revenge for the real shock he put me through. I teased him for that, but I'm not particularly mad at him. Okay, it's time to drop this.

Faster than I can change the subject, Lex drops into a deep bow. "I have been deeply reflecting on my reckless actions that had caused you such dismay, Lady Mizuha. I am sincerely sorry for what I have done…!"

"H-Hang on, hang on! Doing that in public will only draw unwanted attention!"

Case in point, many people around us stop what they're doing to shoot us suspicious looks.

"No! Your knight Lex Irvine shall not back down until he receives Lady Mizuha's pardon!"

# Another World's Zombie Apocalypse Is Not My Problem!

Lex is totally serious, unlike me. And that's exactly why this is in bad taste.

"Okay! I understand your point of view, so stand up already!"

"Pardon my rudeness, but I cannot accept your pity!"

"I'm really not angry at you!"

"Then you forgive me, m'lady?!"

"I forgive you! I *forgive* you!"

"...Thank you very much!" He finally rises.

Sheesh, I better be careful when I tease Lex in the future. At the very least, I'd better pick my spot. Having gained control of the situation for now, I sigh with relief.

"MiZUha...? Are you not, MiZUha?!"

I know of only one person who says my name in such a funny way. I can't believe he's showing up at a time like this. I look in the direction of that voice, feeling like a teacher just sprung a surprise test on me. The young man—Keith—welcomes my look with a pointlessly sparkly smile.

"What a coincidence, running into you here. Or mayhap, it's fate."

"You're launching right into that drivel the second you open your mouth, huh?"

"You look down, MiZUha."

*Because I ran into you of all people.*

"Would you like to join me for a meal?"

"I heard none of the restaurants are open yet."

"How about a stroll, then?"

"Sorry, I want to take it easy today."

"It can't be helped, then. How about you join me at m-m-m-my m-mansion...?!"

*What can't be helped? Huh? Besides that, I seriously wish you'd not sidle up to me with a face that's got your ulterior motives written all over it plain as day. Yick.*

As I'm stuck between being exasperated and totally turned off, Lex smoothly steps between me and Keith.

"You are troubling Lady Mizuha, Lord Rowadan."

"How am I troubling her? She looks terribly delighted to me."

"No, not the least bit delighted," I say, bluntly letting him have the truth. Unfortunately, Keith seems to possess the inconvenient skill of allowing what I say go clean in one ear and out the other, for he looks unfazed by my curt rejection. To make matters worse, he's even threatening Lex, who's blocking his way to me.

"You were here, Lex Irvine?"

"Yes, the whole time."

"I see. Is that what's going on here? MiZUha is dispirited because of your presence!"

Taking him seriously, Lex turns an unconfident gaze my way. "Is that…true?"

"No. Relax, it's not true at all."

"You heard what the lady said."

"To protect this failure of a knight… How kind MiZUha must be."

It's no use. Nothing I say gets through this guy's thick head.

"So be it. MiZUha and I are about to set off on a journey of *love*. Go somewhere else, fly."

"I cannot do that."

"You dare continue to interfere? I've looked into you. Turns out you have no connection to MiZUha whatsoever, fly. Do you have fair reason to stand in my way?"

"I do," Lex asserts, proudly tapping his chest. "After all, I have become Lady Mizuha's official knight."

"Wh-What did you just say…?"

"I am Lady Mizuha's knight, Lex Irvine."

Is it just me hearing that hint of pride in his voice? I don't know Keith's true intentions, but he's definitely suffering a great deal of damage from that admittance. He looks imploringly at me with misty eyes like he still can't believe it.

"Does he speak the truth, MiZUha?"

"Y-Yes, for now."

"AUGH." Keith falls to his knees. I hope he'll give up now. But I guess I thought that too soon, because he bounces back on his feet—literally and figuratively. "I will never, ever give up! You hear me, LEX IRVINE?!"

"I am a knight. I shall neither run nor hide."

Overwhelmed by Lex's imposing confidence, Keith resentfully says nothing more. He turns his back on us and runs.

"He never learns."

"Lady MiZUha…"

## Another World's Zombie Apocalypse Is Not My Problem!

"Lex, you've picked up his weird way of saying my name."

Lex smiles wryly as he looks in the direction Keith left. "A mind of steel. It is one of Lord Rowadan's good points as well as bad."

"Whoa. Don't tell me you acknowledge him now?"

"No, that was the nicest thing I could come up with after racking my brain."

Lex can say some pretty cruel stuff too. Then again, since I'm of the same opinion, I agree with him. "You can say that again."

"Good grief... I guess I should be thankful the holy priestess is easy to find," an exasperated voice says directly behind me. I turn around to find just who I expected to be there.

"Pino!"

"I see you continue to excel at drawing attention."

"Ahaha... It's a coincidence. A coincidence, I say." Ninety percent of it is Keith's fault. "Anyway, what are you doing here? It's rare for you to come all this way."

"I had something I need to tell you now, so I looked for you myself."

"Could it be—"

"Yeah," he nods. "I've pinned down where the black fog is coming from."

## ◆Chapter 21: Quest to Vanquish the Dark Djinn

**UNDER** the bright, pounding rays of the sun, Grantz Kingdom's Royal Army is preparing in the plains just outside the capital to embark on a campaign to take down the Dark Djinn. The eighty soldiers composing this campaign makes it bigger than any other expedition undertaken since reclaiming the capital. Because of that, it's awfully noisy for this time of morning.

"More soldiers are coming along than I thought," I mutter to myself, watching over them near the outer gate.

"More isn't necessarily better in this case either."

"Oh, Pino!" Pino had snuck up behind me without my notice. "Good morning," I greet him. He merely nods in return, as unsociable as ever. "What do you mean more isn't better?"

"Foolishly increasing our numbers could fatally increase the number of pawns falling into the enemy's hands. Our advantage in numbers could quickly become our disadvantage."

"Ahh. Good point."

"In the end, we're stuck relying on the only person who can stand against the enemy—Miss Holy Priestess. Do your best not to get everyone killed."

"You make it sound like it's just my problem..."

That being said, Pino is right. I'd love to list off my mountain of complaints, but that won't do anything to change the truth. Above all else, I'm the one who wanted this vanquishing quest to happen. It's too

## Another World's Zombie Apocalypse Is Not My Problem!

late to whine. I exhale and switch modes.

"Anyway, I thought it'd take more time."

"To pinpoint the fog's source?"

"Yeah. You seemed to be having a difficult time with it."

"The Raw Materials Harvesting Expedition was the clincher. It was easy to locate once I narrowed my search based on that hulking blob you happened across. Investigations of the site from a distance have proved my conjecture correct," Pino explains, squeezing the strap of the double carry sack on his shoulder.

"Speaking of which, you're coming, Pino?"

"Obviously."

"It's going to be dangerous, you know?"

"A worthwhile price to pay to see the Dark Djinn with my own eyes."

"Hmm…"

As wise and talented as Pino is, he's still a child. Is it really okay to knowingly bring him to a dangerous place?

"Miss Priestess. Let me be clear—you aren't my guardian or anything of the like."

"Yeah, I know that, but—"

"If you still plan to stop me from going regardless, I will sneak among the ranks and die in front of you."

"Stop it. That's the one thing you should never do." It's scary because he doesn't sound like he's joking.

"You needn't worry. I'll run away as soon as I perceive it's dangerous," Pino informs me in all seriousness after seeing how reluctant I am.

To be fully honest, I want him to stay in the capital, but it is Pino who created this opportunity for me. I can't put my foot down more than I already have.

The sound of dozens of feet breaks into our conversation. I look in that direction to see a group of twenty approaching from the capital city. All are wearing hooded red robes. The vanguard of the group throws back their hood, revealing a fair and beautiful face.

"…Iris?" It's the young woman who abducted me.

"I caught word that you are going on a quest to vanquish the Dark Djinn, Goddess Mizuha. As such, this is a holy war. The Church of Our Lady Mizuha cannot sit on the sidelines and do nothing."

"Don't tell me the people behind you are—"

"Yes, they are the Church of Our Lady Mizuha believers!" Iris proudly introduces the group.

My lips curve into an unforgiving smile. "Say, Iris? Didn't I tell you to stop with this nonsense?"

"Ack...I made a mistake.... This is the Church of Nnn!" Iris amends by rolling the new name from the back of her throat.

"We're the Church of Nnn!" the group behind her insists in support of her claim. What a pitiful excuse. Exasperation is the only reaction I'm left with.

"I see no reason not to let them come."

"Pino...but..."

"We will absolutely become your strength!" Iris firmly asserts.

I've experienced Iris's superhuman strength for myself. She'll definitely be of more use than I will when it comes to a physical fight.

"Fine. But don't be reckless."

"Did you hear the good news, brothers and sisters?! We were bestowed holy permission to partake in this holy war! We shall rain divine punishment down on the Dark Djinn!"

Iris and her group take statues from their double carry sacks and hold them up in the air. No matter how you look at it, they're statues of a high school girl wearing a school uniform. I'm the only person wearing an outfit like that in this world. In other words—

"Hey, that's—"

"Big Sister!"

Only one person calls me that. I spot Cia behind the believers, flanked by Sir Kurt and Sir Julian. Since Lex became my knight, they have been assigned as Cia's temporary guard.

In the few seconds I was distracted by Cia, Iris and her cult disappeared. I search for where they went and see they've joined up with the soldiers. They sure are quick to flee.

"Cia, you came to see me off?"

"Yes!" Contrary to her energetic response, her expression is dark. "I wish I could go with you, though..."

"Everything would fall apart if anything happened to the princess."

"...I know. Please stay safe, Big Sis."

"Thank you for worrying about me. Let's have tea when I get back."

"I'd love to!" Cia exclaims before facing Pino. "Please be careful as well, Master Pino."

"I-I will…"

Pino's as curt as ever, but he's lacking his usual composure. It clicks in an instant after seeing that reaction.

"Hoho," I smirk. "So she's the one."

"Y-You're wrong! I don't know what misconception you're laboring under, but I—"

"Don't sweat it. I won't tell anybody."

"Like I said, I—"

Cia blinks in confusion when she sees Pino lose his cool. "Pardon me, but what are you talking about?"

"Nngh!" Pino turns his back on Cia to hide his bright-red face from view. "I'll head over first… Miss Priestess, I'll get you for this later."

I seem to have taken my teasing too far. I give a strained smile as cold sweat trickles down my back. At a complete loss, Cia tilts her head, bewildered.

"Lady Mizuha, we're all set!" Lex comes for me on Vianta's back. Sounds like the knights and soldiers are ready to go.

I turn and say one last goodbye to Cia. "I'm heading out now. See you later."

"Okay. Please be careful… May Goddess Sadia's divine protection be with you."

**ONLY** a few horses were recovered by purifying the two Boneless Hams. The troops can move only so fast without steeds, which means we still haven't arrived at our destination after two straight hours of marching. Exhaustion is showing on the soldiers' faces.

"I feel bad for taking one of the horses." I'm riding Vianta in front of Lex. Aside from my butt and thighs hurting from bouncing up and down, I'm experiencing little fatigue.

"We don't know what is lying in wait for us. You are helping us by saving your energy now, Lady Mizuha."

"I know, but I still feel bad." It bothers me to be one of the few who can take it easy on the hard trek to our destination.

"Sit with your head held high because you deserve to take a load off during this part," Pino advises. He's in the same position as me on Sir Oden's horse. The difference in size makes them look like father and son.

Sir Oden has his horse trot beside Vianta. "Master Pino is right. You are an exalted person in Grantz Kingdom, Lady Mizuha. No one will complain about you riding in comfort before going into battle."

"My goddess is the Goddess!" a loud voice bellows behind us after Sir Oden's remark. "You aren't just the most important person in Grantz, but in the whole wide world! If anyone dares voice a complaint, your servant Iris shall—"

"Iris, can you shut your trap?"

"Yes'm."

Sir Oden guffaws when he sees Iris wilt. "You're loved."

"Doesn't what she said count as lèse-majesté?"

"I seem to be hard of hearing lately." The corners of Sir Oden's lips curl up. Looks like he's going to overlook what Iris said. I'm relieved. As insane as she is, Iris is still someone who idolizes me. I wouldn't be able to sleep at night if she were arrested.

We enter the forest a short while later. Sunlight is blocked by a canopy of branches and leaves, dimming the surrounding area into a gloomy darkness. The area extending ahead of us is so dark there's almost zero visibility. The thing is, this is no ordinary darkness. I've seen it plenty of times to know—it's the black fog.

"I've never seen it this thick before."

Fear and unrest courses through the soldiers. I can't shake the bad feeling I have either. This fog is clearly different from the other black fog. Suddenly, a bird the size of a human head lands on a nearby dead tree. Rot oozes from its zombified body. After intensely staring at us with red glowing eyes, it flies into the black fog.

Just as I'm thinking how creepy that was, *something* human-shaped steps out of the black fog. It has four limbs and walks on two legs. Human it may appear, but human it is not. The body appears to be formed from rotten clay. But now's not the time to be focusing my attention on figuring out what makes up that *thing*'s body.

"H-How freakin' many of them are there?!"

Around fifty clay zombie dolls are trudging our way from the black fog.

## Another World's Zombie Apocalypse Is Not My Problem!

"Lex, protect Lady Mizuha!" Sir Oden's voice becomes the battle signal. Knights and soldiers intercept the clay dolls with their shields.

"AGHHHHHHHH!" one of the soldiers screams. He rapidly begins rotting from the spot on his arm where the clay doll he was fighting touched him. Zombies are going to propagate from our own men if we don't do something fast.

"Lex!"

"You've got it, m'lady!"

Lex navigates Vianta closer to the soldiers for me to touch the rotting men and clay zombie dolls. Soldiers regain their humanity, while the clay dolls crumble into a pile on the ground. Looks like the clay zombies can be purified by my power just like normal zombies. I take a whiff of my hand to be sure.

"Yuck! It reeks to high heaven!"

"Their appearance and base material is different, but it appears they are zombies just the same," Lex infers, then shouts orders to the troops. "Listen up, men! These clay dolls work the same way as zombies! Whatever you do, don't touch or be touched!"

Our enemies lack fine motor agility. They don't pose much of a threat as long as the troops are careful. I purify the clay zombies knocked down and immobilized by the soldiers. Their numbers took me by surprise at first, but we're down to ten by the time it occurs to me to count again.

"I think we can handle this." I'm taking a short break to wipe the sweat from my brow, when new clay zombies appear from the black fog. And if that wasn't bad enough, it's around the same number as the first time, if not more. My right cheek spasms. "...I *hope* we can handle this."

Thereafter, I purify dozens after dozens of zombies without flinching. Problem is, even after I decrease their numbers, more are ejected from the black fog, resulting in their numbers never diminishing. When even more clay zombies pop out, Lex groans in frustration.

"Grah! More?!"

"I can keep going!"

"Yes, but at this rate there will be no end...!"

My stamina definitely won't keep up if I have to take on a never-ending army of clay zombies. We need to come up with a strategy to break the deadlock. Not that I'm suddenly struck by any such genius idea when I need it. All I can do is survey our surroundings and reconfirm our situation. Meanwhile, another batch of clay zombies is popped out by the black fog.

"I wonder if the zombies will stop showing up if we get rid of that blasted fog."

"It's worth trying," Lex says, responding to my muttered idea.

"But how?"

"By using your powers, of course, Lady Mizuha."

"Right, that's how it's always gotta be, isn't it?"

I knew it. I knew it was going to come to that before he even said it.

"The main problem is how do we make it to where you can touch the fog—"

"Then you have no problem! I shall cut open a path for you!" Sir Oden's thundering voice suddenly cuts into our conversation from where he's fighting nearby. He apparently overheard. He thrusts away the clay zombies he was taking on and holds his shield out in the direction of the black fog.

"Captain of Grantz Kingdom's Royal Knights, Oden Jaxor, hereby charges!" Sir Oden propels forward while howling, driving his shield through the clay zombies in his way and sending them in different directions. Obviously, he isn't holding back like he does with former-human zombies. A path to the black fog is being opened before my eyes.

"Here we go, Lady Mizuha!"

"I'm ready!"

Lex kicks Vianta into an all-out run. I'd expect no less of a warhorse—we're rapidly closing the distance to Sir Oden. However, the closer we get, the narrower our path becomes. The repelled clay zombies have staggered their way back.

"Just a little farther! Hurry, Lex!"

Sir Oden has secured us safe passage to the black fog. Vianta advances, narrowly evading the clay hands reaching for her legs, until we finally reach our destination. Then, out of one of our blind spots, a lone zombie lunges.

It's going to claw Vianta!

My fears leave just as quickly as they came, for Sir Oden charges the zombie with his ginormous shield. He powerfully slams into the clay zombie, knocking it far away.

"GO!"

## Another World's Zombie Apocalypse Is Not My Problem!

"Thanks, Sir Oden!"

Vianta gallops past the rest of the clay zombies until Lex reins her in just alongside the black fog.

"Lady Mizuha, now!"

Even before Lex's call to action, I was stretching my arm out as far as it could go. My fingers brush along the black fog. It feels like nothingness, except exhaustion washes over me like a tidal wave, a reminder that my power has activated. Several seconds later, the black fog unleashes a blinding light, instantly losing all color until it entirely disappears.

Clay zombies crumble where they stand, returning back to the earth from whence they came. Looks like my theory that the black fog was producing an endless supply of clay zombies was on the money.

"It appears we pulled it off."

"Yeah." Reveling in my momentary relief, I turn my attention on the place previously hidden by the black fog. An old log cabin stands there all by its lonesome.

"**WHY** is there a log cabin in a place like this…?"

Everyone, including myself, is staring in disbelief. I'd expected the Dark Djinn to be waiting on the other side of the dispersed fog, so now I feel like someone just pulled a fast one on me.

"Each and every one of you is an annoying pest."

The cabin door opens with a loud creak, and out steps a woman. She appears to be in her forties and has a pretty homely, rustic look going on. Her black hair, long enough to touch the ground, is dull and splitting, and her clothes are not only tattered and in shreds but yellowed from age. In a sense…she almost looks like what would happen if Iris fell even further into the dark side.

"Say, Iris?" I ask over my shoulder. "Is that your mom?"

"She is not!" Iris frantically denies.

"So you're the little brat who keeps getting in my way." The woman shoots me a barbed glare.

"Getting in your way? Are you the one behind the zombies…?" I venture.

"Yes, it is I. I am the one who dyed this world in darkness with Lord Diallo's powers!" she proclaims, throwing her arms wide. She's boasting rather than denying it.

"Pino, who's Diallo?"

"That's the Dark Djinn's name."

By her own account, this woman is definitely connected to the Dark Djinn, and judging by what she's admitted to, she's the perpetrator of this curse. At any rate, we might be able to put an end to this chaos if we capture her.

Meanwhile, Sir Oden is scrunching up his face behind Pino for some reason. "I feel like I've seen her face before…" he mutters while stroking his beard, and then his eyes fly wide open. "I remember now! She's the woman who used to stalk His Majesty! I think her name was Jela!"

"What lies are you spouting, old goat?!" Jela bites back less than a second later.

"O-Old goat?!"

She speaks over Sir Oden's consternation. "Stalked? I did no such thing. I was merely trying to inform His Regalness of the truth."

I assume His Regalness refers to Cia's dad—the king.

"The truth?" Sir Oden repeats. Jela nods.

"Yes. The truth about how that Lia woman was deceiving him. That wench approached him for money. She's a devil who wormed her way into His Regalness's magnanimous heart."

"You're the one deceiving yourself, lady. His Majesty is the one who fell for Her Majesty first and set up their meeting."

"Lies! If he was going to pick a commoner as queen, he would've picked me! I mean, I'm far, far more beautiful than she is!"

Keeping one eye on Jela as she goes into hysterics, I quietly confirm the situation with Lex. "Sooo, she was just jealous?"

"So it seems."

"Holy smokes…"

To involve the Dark Djinn and the world in her jealousy—Jela's a woman to be feared. She whirls on me with a vengeful look.

"It's not JEALOUSY, I say!" she shrieks in an ear-piercing voice. My ears are painfully ringing. "Forget you pestilences! Nuisances! Nuisances!" She's raking her hands through her hair and pulling at it from the roots. "I'm in the middle of enjoying my life with His Regalness

## Another World's Zombie Apocalypse Is Not My Problem!

too! Your presence here has caused me to waste minutes of my precious time with him!"

"Does that mean His Majesty is here?!"

Jela answers Sir Oden's question with her lips curled. "Yes, he is. His Regalness is living with me. You could say this is our love nest."

Who would have thought the king was quarantined here all this time? No wonder we never found him among the city zombies.

"Cia's dad is in there… Lex!"

"Yes, m'lady!" Lex pulls on the reins, drawing an eager neigh from Vianta. Sir Oden and the rest of the troops fall into battle readiness.

"You look all hot and ready to see some action, but have your flea brains already forgotten I have Lord Diallo's powers?!" Jela drops on all fours and lets a wad of spit roll down her tongue.

After seeing that, Lex cries out, "Sh-She does the same act as Lady Mizuha?!"

"I don't do that!"

I seriously wish he wouldn't lump me in with her… Though I do spit on the ground.

Before we finish conversing, the saliva rolls off Jela's tongue and hits the ground. Black fog surges up and blankets the land.

"Now go, my lovely! Protect our love nest!"

No sooner do bulges protrude from the ground than *something* bursts from it like an explosion. A fraction of a second later, darkness befalls the area, but not because of black fog. That SOMETHING is just so friggin' big it's blocking out the sun.

"BWOOOOHHHHH!"

A ginormous zombie stands in front of us.

## ◆Chapter 22: Divine Punishment!

"**YOU'VE** gotta be freakin' kidding me!"

Giganta-zombie stands over a good thirty-five feet tall. It's way, way bigger than Boneless Ham. Naturally, its feet are large enough to hold up all that bulk and will undoubtedly turn us into splatter pancakes if it steps on us.

"Get that little brat! The world will return to being ours if she's taken out of the picture!"

"It just had to be me, didn't it?!"

I knew it. I so knew it, but never have I wished so hard in my life that I was wrong. Lex kicks his feet against Vianta's flank, pulling tight on her reins to change direction. KA-BAM! KA-BAM! KA-BAM! Footsteps that sound more like small explosions follow right behind us. Vianta is doing her best, but Giganta-zombie is only getting closer.

If someone could just take Jela down while her pet's preoccupied!

My slim hopes are dashed by the woman being smarter than she looks—two clay zombies are protecting her on both sides. Black fog swirls around them, giving them a different aura from the clay zombies we fought earlier.

Meanwhile, Giganta-zombie bends down and sweeps out its right arm. I crush myself as close to Vianta's back as I can go under Lex. Cracking, creaking, and snapping noises—the sound of trees and branches being mowed down—blare around me. The massive shadow passes over our heads. We just barely escaped a direct hit.

We are, however, hit by the raging gust that directly followed the

## Another World's Zombie Apocalypse Is Not My Problem!

attack. I'm knocked off balance, but Lex's arms hold me up, preventing me from falling off Vianta. After a relieved breath, I shoot a weary look behind me. Giganta-zombie is still gunning for us.

"It'll catch up at this rate!"

I don't know what face Lex is making because he's behind me, but his silence speaks volumes—he has no good ideas.

"Miss Priestess!" calls a young voice unbefitting of the battlefield. Sir Oden has his horse, with Pino on it, gallop parallel to Vianta.

"Pino?!"

"Go to that cabin! It shouldn't be able to attack there!"

Jela did call that place her "love nest." She'll surely stop her Giganta-zombie from destroying it. I feel bad for putting the king in danger, but at the rate we're going, my only other future is being squashed or catapulted to my doom.

"Lex!"

"As you command!"

Vianta reverses directions again. Giganta-zombie is so close I can see it only from the waist down, which makes me realize just how big it is all over again. I just know if I were using my own legs, I'd be too scared to run. I'm glad from the bottom of my heart that I'm riding Vianta. Or at least I was, until now. I wish she'd stop! Why is she running straight at Giganta-zombie?!

"Hey! Why aren't you going around it?! We're gonna die! DIEEEEEEEEE!"

"We are going to break through between its legs!"

"NOOOOOOOOOOOOOOOOOOOOOOOOOOOOOOOOOOO!"

Giganta-zombie lifts its right leg to stomp on us. A building-sized foot is descending over my head. A few seconds more and we'll be literal toast—and we pass through just before that happens. As the ground shakes like an earthquake, we pass by the zombie's left leg, which had become its pivot leg.

"My heaaarrt…"

My heart is hammering in my chest. The monstrous strength of Giganta-zombie makes this my closest call yet.

"You little ants! Hurry and smash them, my lovely!" Jela's orders send Giganta-zombie into a frenzy after us.

We had distanced ourselves from that love-nest cabin during our previous escape. It'll take some time to get back to it. That might give her enough time to figure out our plan to use the cabin as a shield and come up with a counterplan.

My fears are needless, though, because Sir Oden starts shouting at Jela, distracting her. "Listen to me, Jela or whatever you call yourself! You've probably blinded yourself to it, but His Majesty and Queen Lia were a very intimate and loving couple! So loving that they have gone down in history as the ultimate husband-wife team since Grantz Kingdom was founded!"

I get it. He's trying to get under her skin by forcing her to hear about the king and queen's lovey-dovey relationship. Oddly enough, it doesn't have as much of an effect on Jela as I had thought.

"Are you trying to provoke me?! I won't fall for such a cheap trick!"

"Allow me to relate to you the special words His Majesty used to propose to Lady Lia that I wheedled out of him when he was drunk! Ahem! 'You are more beautiful than any other! In heart, mind, and body! I would have found you no matter how far you may have been from me—'"

"Damn old goat! Don't lie through your yellow teeth! There's no way that cow was more beautiful than me! I'll kill you!"

For a moment, I feared his plan wouldn't work, but it turned out to be easier than expected to get Jela worked up. While she is getting all "passionate" over Sir Oden, we almost get within reach of the so-called love nest. Being noticed won't be a problem for us now. Actually, not being noticed will be the problem.

"Hey! Lady! Is it okay for Giganta-zombie here to keep going like this?!" I call out.

"HUH?! Of course it's okay! Yes, keep going, my lovely! Crush that little twerp underfoot— Ack! No, it's not okay! Wait! HOLD UP! MY LOVE NEEEEEEEST!"

Giganta-zombie's already-lifted foot stops midair as Jela shrieks. It's my little secret that my heart nearly jumped out of my chest when she didn't notice what was happening right away. Jela exhales, thoroughly relieved that she stopped her pet in time too.

Vianta uses that opening to gallop over to Giganta-zombie's massive foot.

## Another World's Zombie Apocalypse Is Not My Problem!

"Take this!"

I smack my right hand along that foot. Blinding light radiates from the gigantic three-story-house-sized body. The sheer size of the zombie means the light covers the whole area in bright white.

Too bad I can still clearly hear Jela's deranged shrieks of "You tricked meeeee, twerrrrrrrp!"

As the light disperses, seams run over Giganta-zombie's body like the outlines of puzzle pieces. Each piece falls away, and a variety of animals roll out, dropping onto the ground like it's literally raining cats and dogs. Every animal is covered in a thick pink mucus. My stomach turns just looking at that slime; if I can avoid it, I'd rather not go near them.

"Blurgh," I throw up a little in my mouth.

"For a moment, I thought we were doomed…" Lex admits.

"We somehow made it through," I agree, holding my hand over my mouth to stop from puking.

"Indeed. All thanks to Vianta here." Lex gently strokes Vianta's neck.

All of a sudden, the clay zombies guarding Jela rush at us with breakneck speed. They close the distance crawling on all fours across the ground and wrap around Vianta's legs. Spooked, Vianta bucks wildly, throwing both Lex and me off.

"Lady Mizuha!"

Lex protectively hurls himself under me. Thanks to quick thinking on his part, my body doesn't slam into the ground, but greater danger is already upon us. One of the black fog–shrouded clay zombies lunges for my throat. Lex brandishes his already-drawn sword, intercepting the attack.

"Lex!"

The clay zombie's onslaught has a lot of weight behind it. Lex's face is twisting with the strain. I have to get in there and purify the zombie before—

My thoughts are interrupted by an imminent attack.

"Everything will go back to the way it was if I kill you!" Jela, propelled from behind by the black fog, slips past Lex and is heading straight at me. Her long, sharp bladelike claws are within inches of my throat. She's coming in so fast I can't escape.

Why now?! We've come so close!

Resigned to die, I slam my eyes shut. A dull thud comes immediately after. What in the zombie apocalypse happened?! I promptly open my eyes to find Jela collapsed on the ground in front of me. Out of the corner of my vision I see a statue of a high school girl—by which I mean a statue of me—rolling on the ground. Could it be—

"Divine punishment!" declares a clear, sonorous voice. In the direction of that voice stands Iris with her head held high and proud, triumph in her eyes.

**Another World's Zombie Apocalypse Is Not My Problem!**

## ◆Chapter 23: The Real One Appears

"SHEESH, I told you not to hurt other people anymore."

"How could I not when this old hag was trying to kill my goddess—"

"Don't means don't."

"Boooo…"

After lecturing Iris where she sits kneeling on the ground, I exhale a small breath and change tack. "But you did save me, so…" I pat her on the head just the way she likes. "Thank you. Honestly, I might've died if you hadn't intervened, Iris."

"Ehehe… Iris is being shown favor," she purrs.

It's anyone's guess if she actually understands, but it's true she saved my life. I'll spoil her to bits to show my gratitude. As I'm gently patting her on the head, the other believers timidly approach.

"E-Excuse me… W-we also threw goddess statues! So!"

"So?"

"Erm, a patting…"

I narrow my eyes on the group of restlessly fidgeting believers.

"Were you not listening to me earlier? I told you it was dangerous. And anyway, it's way too risky if everyone throws them at the same time! It's a good thing they all missed aside from Iris's…"

"Tch! We shall practice throwing starting tomorrow—"

"Don't."

"Yes'm."

They're an unstable group from beginning to end. I overlooked it before, but a complete crackdown on them might be necessary for the world and all the people in it. Sighing, I glance toward the unconscious Jela being tied up with rope by the soldiers. Just to be safe, I healed her with my left hand, so we shouldn't have to worry about her injuries.

"I found him! I found His Majesty!" Lex calls out from the "love nest"—also known as the rundown cabin. I had him scout it out first to determine if it's safe. I go inside with Pino and Sir Oden.

"It's crazy dusty in here."

"The stench of mold is overpowering too."

With only a plain desk and a chair covered in cobwebs, the cabin shockingly lacks any signs of being lived in. I'd never want to live in a place like this for any amount of time. It's in the corner of this drab shack that we find Lex. He's holding up a horribly emaciated man.

"Your Majesty!" Sir Oden rushes over to the gaunt man as if coal had been lit under his feet. Judging by that reaction, this man is unquestionably Grantz's king.

The king's parched, cracked lips slowly part. "Oden. You've done well coming here…"

"I couldn't have done it without the others, sire."

"Cia… Is Cia safe?"

"Yes, sire. She is safely waiting back at the castle."

"…Is she?" No sooner does the king crack a relieved smile than his expression turns serious. "Incidentally, Oden, did you enjoy announcing my once-in-a-lifetime proposal for all to hear? Hmm?"

"…Your Majesty, it appears you haven't fully regained consciousness yet. Please rest comfortably until we return to the castle—"

"*Oden.* Be prepared for consequences later."

"Y-Yes, sire…"

Even the brave and mighty Sir Oden is like putty before his king. Pino and I are quietly laughing when the king shifts his gaze to another corner of the room. A staircase descends from there.

"Below is Lia…and the Dark Djinn."

"Please leave the rest to us, sire," Lex soothes. Mind set at ease, the king's eyes close. He's lost consciousness. Lex entrusts the king to the other knights and rises to his feet. "Let's do this."

## Another World's Zombie Apocalypse Is Not My Problem!

**ONLY** two candles are burning in the cellar. It's too poorly lit to make out every corner of the room. Then I see it—a lone woman chained to the wall like she's being crucified there.

"Queen Lia!" Lex dashes over to her.

This woman must be Cia's mom. She does share the same hair color, and I can see some similar facial features. Unlike the king, however, she is covered in blistering injuries. The wounds are so grotesque, I instinctively look away.

"Lady Mizuha."

"Right."

My healing ability does nothing for recovering stamina or curing disease, but it is capable of healing wounds. I place my left hand on Queen Lia and watch as the deep cuts carved into her body heal before my eyes. She hasn't regained consciousness, but her breathing sounds calmer now.

"Jela lost, then?" inquires a voice that sounds like an ensemble of overlapping bass notes. An obscured shadow sways in the deepest part of the room where the voice came from. The shadow's outline is hard to make out, but it has a humanlike shape.

Lex and Sir Oden draw their swords.

"Sheathe your blades. I don't have the strength to resist you now."

"...Another one of your tricks, monster?"

Contrary to Sir Oden going on high alert, Pino is calm. "That stupid woman failed to revive you in full?"

"I see the tiny one is capable of holding a conversation."

Pino snorts. His snotty attitude doesn't fail him even before the Dark Djinn. "Or perhaps it's more accurate to say you could only use your power through her as a conduit? It's no wonder your attacks were laughable."

"You would not be standing here if I were whole. Nay, Sadia never even let me net a countermeasure against her." In the middle of the swaying shadow, two purple glowing balls I assume are eyes pierce through me. "Oi, you there."

"M-Me?"

"Is there anyone but you who received Sadia's powers, woman?"

Pino once ran the idea by me that my powers might belong to the Goddess, and it seems he was right.

"Get this over with."

"Get what over with…?"

"Purification. What else?"

I stare blankly at the shadow. "Uh, are you sure? Don't you want to fight it out or something first?"

"I'd much rather vanish than be stuck in this shitty state."

Well, that's sportsmanlike of him. It's surprising after the underhanded, sinister picture I had arbitrarily painted of him in my mind. Maybe the Dark Djinn isn't so bad after all? That stupid thought briefly crosses my mind, but I shake it right out of my head. The zombie apocalypse would've never befallen this world if not for this malevolent deity. He doesn't need my sympathy.

I walk over to the Dark Djinn and reach out my right hand. "P-Pardon me, then."

"…Oi, woman. I won't go easy on you next time," he threatens.

I was so stupid for thinking for even a second that he might not be evil. That proves it—he's wicked through and through. Letting out a small cry, I stretch across the final distance and touch the Dark Djinn's shadow. The darkness around the back of the room pulses, until the light created by my right hand completely erases it.

When the blinding light filling the room finally fades, I open my eyes along with the others. A frighteningly beautiful woman is left standing in the back of the room. She in no way looks like she's someone of this world. A halo of light radiates from behind her, giving credence to that idea.

"Thank you all for what you have done," the woman says in a clear, bell-like voice.

"Mayhap…you are Goddess Sadia?" Sir Oden asks in a trembling voice.

"Such appears to be the name you call me among your people."

Sir Oden and Lex sigh in awe at her response. Even the all-knowing Pino appears taken by surprise. As for me, I'm not all that shocked. Perhaps because I could sense she was the Goddess the moment she appeared.

"Excuse me, I have a question… Are you the one who brought me to this world, Goddess?" I ask her the number-one question I wanted to ask should we ever meet.

## Another World's Zombie Apocalypse Is Not My Problem!

Her expression drops into a doleful smile. "Yes. I have put you through much strife."

"You sure have. You chucked me into a post-apocalyptic world full of nothing but zombies... I was nearly killed, then mistaken for a goddess and confined to a creepy hellhole against my will."

"Ulp!"

"Ah, I'm not blaming you for it. Sure, I had to humiliate myself on a constant basis, since the only way to purify water was by spitting in it. But I don't blame you one BIT for that."

"Ummm..." Goddess Sadia is gradually shrinking in on herself.

"Merciless," Pino whispers.

She put me through a hell of an experience, but I don't actually resent her for it. This is just my passive-aggressive way of getting back at her.

"I just wish you had explained things to me first," I huff.

"I-I'm sorry. It took everything I had just to summon you to this world and bestow my powers upon you."

"But why me? I know it sounds weird for me to say this, but I'm sure there's a more suitable person than me."

Goddess Sadia gives a placating smile as she slowly shakes her head. "No, there is none but you. Your heart is closest to mine."

"I'm...similar to you?"

I don't have some pure and noble heart like a saint. Even so, being told I'm akin to a goddess not only doesn't sound half bad, it makes me a little happy too. As I'm reveling in self-satisfaction, someone pops their head out around my shoulder.

"See! My goddess is the Goddess after all! Iris wasn't wrong!"

"Iris?! I told you to wait outside!"

"Eep. I was curious about the immense light spilling from inside..."

"Shut your mouth and keep quiet."

"Yes'm!" Iris drops to her knees and covers her mouth with both hands.

She always kicks up a loud fuss when it comes to the Goddess. I had her wait outside because I thought something like this might happen, but it looks like my efforts were in vain.

"I have something to ask you," Pino enquires of Goddess Sadia with a hard expression. "Did Diallo take control because your powers were waning? I just can't fathom that stupid woman having enough power to wake Diallo up."

"You have guessed correctly. Torstana and Ladan are the main causes."

As that conversation is going on, I whisper my question to Lex. "Hey, what are Torstana and Ladan?"

"Two major powers on par with Grantz. Both countries have been at war for decades."

Cia once told me about two countries that were currently engaged in hostilities, and it seems these are the ones.

"That's what I thought. But I can't believe a being worshipped as a god is influenced by what's going on in the world."

Goddess Sadia offers a troubled smile in reply to Pino's cynicism. It's fine for him to be fearless and all, but he should at least be respectful to a goddess.

"The world should slowly purify itself now that I am back in control."

"It won't just come back at the snap of a finger?" I venture.

"As your friend mentioned, my powers are in a weakened state right now." Goddess Sadia turns her attention to me, then changes the subject. "Now then, you successfully fulfilled your duties. If you so desire it, I shall send you back to your own world this instant."

This was the topic I'd been hesitating to bring up myself. Really, though, I just wanted to know if it was possible to go back—I still haven't made the final decision about what I want to do yet.

I look askance at Lex and our eyes meet. At first, his expression is a complex mix of emotions, but a smile immediately rises to the surface. He's supporting my decision. I know that. I know it, but—

"Excuse me! Is it possible for you to hold off for a bit?"

"Lady Mizuha?!" Lex cries in disbelief.

"Ah, well, how do I put it? It's all happening too soon."

Lex's surprise is reasonable, considering I've only ever spoken to him about going home. I'm starting to feel uncomfortable, so I shift my gaze back to Goddess Sadia to avoid looking at Lex.

"I am presently capable of speaking and using my power of my own volition. However, my existence is normally a part of the world. All my powers are used to maintain world order."

"In other words, you won't have the leeway to send me home after

### Another World's Zombie Apocalypse Is Not My Problem!

this?"

"At least not until the entire world has been purified of the zombie blight."

How much time will it take for the whole world to be cleansed? I can't even begin to estimate it. The one thing I do know is that Goddess Sadia is weak. It'll definitely take an extraordinary amount of time.

"I am responsible for dragging you into my world's problems. I shall do whatever it takes to keep my present form for a whole day."

Meaning, I have to come up with my answer by then.

"I have yet to ask your name."

"...I'm Mizuha."

"I am the last person you wish to hear this from, but…please think it over carefully, *Mizuha*. This decision will drastically alter your future."

## ◆Chapter 24: A Lot Has Happened

IT'S the night of our triumphal return to the capital.

"How are they?" I ask Cia as she steps out of the king's bedchamber. Pino, beside me, is waiting for her answer too.

"They have regained consciousness. They can't walk yet, but I think they should be just fine with time."

"I see. Glad to hear it!" Wholehearted relief washes over me. Though I had healed them, the king and queen were in a considerably emaciated state. I'm really glad to hear they're pulling through.

Cia drops into a deep bow. "Big Sister…I am thankful to you beyond words."

"I only smacked some zombies around. It's the people who came with me who did all the heavy lifting. We were able to take out the Giganta-zombie mostly thanks to Pino's quick thinking."

"Is that so? I would expect no less from our master scholar, Pino."

"D-Don't mention it. I simply offered advice."

"No, I cannot let your deeds go unrecognized." Cia shakes her head and wraps both hands around Pino's right hand. "Thank you very much. I will repay you for this favor someday."

"Y-You do that…" Pino is stiffer than a pole. He's so transparent.

"Um…Big Sister…" Cia steps away from Pino and looks questioningly to me.

"You don't have to say it. You want to stay with your parents right now, I'm sure."

"I still can't believe they are back with me."

### Another World's Zombie Apocalypse Is Not My Problem!

"Go. Be with them. Your presence will surely be reassuring to them both."

"Thank you!"

That's a good smile. Cia must be over the moon about her parents' return.

"If you will excuse me here, then," she says in parting before returning to the king's bedchamber.

Taking advantage of being alone with Pino now, I turn on him with a teasing grin.

"...What is that face for?"

"Hmm? Nothing!"

"I don't know what nonsense your brain has come up with this time, but I think nothing of her."

"Sure, let's leave it at that."

Pino clicks his tongue. Then he sighs and becomes serious. "Enough games. Are you sure you don't want to tell her?"

"Hmm? Tell her what?"

"Playing dumb?"

I haven't told Cia about Goddess Sadia pressuring me into deciding whether I want to go home now or not.

"Thanks," I say in place of a direct answer.

"Hmph. It has nothing to do with me. Well, I may find myself a tad bored if you do go, but…it's your life. Do with it what you will," he spits, turning his back on me and stalking away.

I smile dryly as I watch his small back retreat. "Someone's not honest with himself."

I'VE come to the garden located on the tower keep's third floor. I rest my arms on the balustrade and look out over the capital city. With the essential rule of keeping the lights out still in effect, not a single flame can be seen. My eyes seem to have adapted enough to make out the faint outline of buildings.

"Is this where you have been, m'lady?" someone asks from behind me. The voice belongs to Lex; I can tell without looking. "You are going to catch a cold."

"Let me stay here a little longer."

"...Have you found your answer?"

To whether I'm staying or going.

"I've been thinking all this time about what's happened since I arrived here." The night breeze blows, tousling my hair. I push it up and over my ears. "I woke up to a poisonous lake and a stench worse than anything I've smelled before. Before I could figure out my left from right, a zombie showed up. It was nothing but horrifying surprise after horrifying surprise."

"To this day I have not forgotten that powerful blow to my chest."

"Wh-What other choice did I have? You came at me out of nowhere!"

At the time, he stunk so bad I could barely hold it together. I was just desperate to get him away from me.

"However, that was the occasion that let us know you have the power of purification, Lady Mizuha."

"What happened after that was the worst of the worse."

"Your saliva?"

"It still embarrasses me to no end. Thanks to a certain someone, people like to call me the Holy Priestess of Spit."

"They mean it as a title of honor, not an insult, m'lady."

"Which makes it even worse..." I groan.

Grantz Kingdom is full of folks with more than a few screws loose, but they're all good people anyway.

"Then I met Cia and headed for the capital, but... Here's a question for you. I believe we did something INCREDIBLY reckless and foolish next, but, in retrospect, what do you think about that bright idea of yours, Sir Lex Irvine?"

"Th-That is...something I am reflecting on for my rash miscalculation."

"You should be. All's well that ends well, but we could've very easily been overwhelmed and turned into zombies at that point."

"...I have no excuse."

I don't blame him as much as my words and tone make it sound like I do. He just put me through the scare of a lifetime, so this is my way of getting back at him.

"Well, we still managed to regain the castle despite a stupid plan. It's what happened afterward that took me by real surprise."

## Another World's Zombie Apocalypse Is Not My Problem!

"No one had any idea the zombies become extremely active at night."

"You can say that again. I'm really lucky to have escaped to a safe place with my life."

Memories of taking the secret passage from Cia's bedchamber flood my mind, the most poignant memory being Lex's broad back as he blocked the zombies from knocking down the door. And then there's the moment I returned to her bedchamber to find him protecting the secret passage despite turning into a zombie.

"You were kind of cool then, Lex."

"...Desperation was all I had going for me. Desperation that I had to protect you both no matter the cost."

"Thanks."

"No thanks necessary."

Another case of this being the natural course of action for a knight.

"Things finally calmed down enough after that for me to purify and increase our numbers exponentially."

"Though other problems did crop up just when we thought things were going smoothly. Such as the appearance of thieves."

"Like Rosso? Personally, I thought being abducted by Iris had more of an impact."

"I can never apologize enough for that one."

"It's all good. You rescued me in the end."

If you had told me at the time about how well-behaved Iris would become, I wouldn't have believed it. She occasionally—or rather, always if unwatched—goes off the deep end.

"A lot has happened over a short time."

"...Indeed, m'lady."

"I'll be honest with you—lots of horrible things having to do with stenches and ever-present zombies happened, but to an equal degree— No, even more so than that, I've met a lot of great people."

There's Lex, Cia, Sir Oden, and Pino, as well as Rosso, Iris, Sir Kurt, and Sir Julian. I met even more incredible people during the handshake sessions too. My circle of friends has extended much further than I could have ever imagined back on Earth.

"It was fun. It was a ton of fun, actually. I'm glad from the bottom of my heart that I came to this world." I look over my shoulder and convey those feelings with a smile. There's no real reason; I just felt the desire to tell Lex to his face. "Okay, it's time for me to sleep."

"Very well. Good night, Lady Mizuha." I walk past Lex, heading for the pillared corridor. "Lady Mizuha!" he abruptly yells.

I turn back to find him looking torn and flustered. I tilt my head. "Yes?"

"No…never mind." Lex averts his eyes as he chews his bottom lip. He's trembling. His hands are clenched into fists. What is Lex thinking right now? If I don't have the complete wrong idea, it must be—

I take a small breath and pull my smile back up. "Can I trust my guard detail to you again tomorrow?"

"…Yes, of course you can, m'lady."

**Another World's Zombie Apocalypse Is Not My Problem!**

## ◆Chapter 25: Even a Zombie-Filled World Can Be Good

**THE** next morning, I mount Vianta with Lex and ride to where Goddess Sadia is waiting. No one else is with us. Vanquishing the Dark Djinn drastically reduced the danger outside the city walls, removing the need to have a small squad of guards trailing after us.

I haven't spoken to Lex today beyond the bare minimum conversation necessary to do what needs to be done. Because of that, I can hear Vianta's hooves hitting the ground and the rustling leaves clear as day. Not long after entering the forest, we come upon the area where big trees have been cruelly ripped from the ground, knocked over, and split as if a tornado had passed through. Car-sized dents mar the ground in various locations. This is where Giganta-zombie rampaged yesterday.

Beyond the downed trees is Jela's cabin. Lex ties Vianta to a nearby tree and helps me down.

"I wonder if she's in the cellar still," I say aloud, breaking the silence between us.

"Good question."

As soon as I open the cabin door, I'm blinded by a searing light. "Yeow!" I cry, reflexively covering my eyes with my arm.

"You arrived sooner than expected."

Slowly lowering my arm, I see Goddess Sadia where the light had been. She's sitting with her legs crossed, elegantly sipping tea from the dainty teacup in her hand. A sweet, floral fragrance hangs in the air as though to demonstrate that she is drinking a delicious first-class black tea.

"...You seem to be very relaxed," Lex quietly observes.

"W-Well, I had too much free time on my hands, so..." Goddess Sadia quickly returns her teacup to its saucer on the desk and gives a discomfited smile.

I certainly didn't expect to find this world's goddess twiddling away the time drinking tea, regardless of how little there is to do out here in the middle of nowhere. I'm just hankering to ask her where the tea came from. I stare at her hard.

"You said it'd be hard for you to hang around, but it looks to me like you're holding up just fine."

"That isn't necessarily true. I am just barely enduring this as it is." She pulls her shoulders back and sits up straight to maintain her dignified demeanor. Goddess Sadia might be worldlier than I thought. Made uncomfortable by my exasperated, pointed stare, she rises to her feet. "E-Enough about me! ...Care to tell me your answer now?"

She suddenly brings the conversation to a head. "Yes," I say. I arrived at the answer yesterday. I have nothing left to hesitate over. "My original world—"

"Lady Mizuha!" Lex interrupts, his shout so loud and abrupt that I flinch.

"...L-Lex?"

"F-Forgive me." Just when I think he's lowered his head, Lex lifts his chin and looks at me with seriousness gleaming in his eyes. "You have your own world, Lady Mizuha. I know that. Knights are meant to serve their masters. I am fully aware my conduct right now would normally never be allowed. However, even so, I..." After a three-second pause, he finishes with quiet firmness, "Wish to be at your side, Lady Mizuha."

I'm struck by the feeling of something piercing through me. Lex's gorgeous sapphire eyes are peering right into the depths of my soul. It's kind of embarrassing. But I can't take my eyes off him.

"If you are going to return to your world, Lady Mizuha, I shall accompany you there. Please allow me to come with you!"

"Lex..."

I never knew he was this attached to me. His oath to serve as my knight means more to him than I realized; it's taken root in his heart and has manifested in his conduct.

## Another World's Zombie Apocalypse Is Not My Problem!

"That cannot be done," Goddess Sadia says in my place, bluntly rejecting him. A shadow instantly falls over Lex's gallant face.

"…Why not?"

"I'm the last person who has any right to speak of this after bringing her to this world, but transporting people between worlds is fundamentally taboo. I cannot break the taboo again to send you with her."

"This cannot be true… Then what am I— What should I do…?!" Lex drops his gaze and shakes his head. Anguish painfully coats his voice.

I, however, do not feel the same sense of loss and urgency as he does. After all, I never thought of this moment as a lifelong separation. Feeling slightly guilty, I speak to him as gently as possible.

"I'm a little perplexed by this unexpected turn of events, but…hear me out, Lex."

"…Yes, m'lady?"

"I don't plan to go back, you know?"

"Is that…so? So it should be. It is only natural for you to care more about the world you were born and raised in. You would be ill in the head to grow attached to and think about lingering in a world you were in for only a few months— Wait! Did you say you are staying?!" After having his head stuck in the clouds for a few long moments, he finally catches on.

"Yeah. Sorry I'm ill in the head."

"Ah, don't be. About that part…I can only apologize. More importantly! Are you really, truly, positively staying?!"

"Yeah."

"Wh-Why…?"

He still can't believe it. To be perfectly honest, a part of me doesn't believe it either. But this is what I had decided after thinking it through.

"I agree with you that it's stranger to choose staying over going. While we have succeeded in purifying the zombies around Grantz's capital city, this is still a rotten, post-apocalyptic world full of zombies. Frankly, the food, clothes, and shelter in my world are a thousand times better than what's here."

"Then is that not even more reason to—"

"But how can I explain it? I've grown attached? Or something like that. Partly it's that I want to enjoy the environment I've finally secured after all the painful and scary experiences I went through. As I've watched Grantz Kingdom work toward restoration, it hit me that I'm a part of this place as well."

What I want to do with my life—I've always hoped I'd figure out what that is. I've slowly gone through life without finding it—until now. Not that I had expected to find my purpose in another world, and one that has the worst possible circumstances to boot.

I'm the most surprised by my decision because I've always played it safe, avoiding trouble at any cost for my entire life. But I don't regret this choice.

"But then you won't get to see your family again..." Lex sadly reminds me.

"As for that part..." I face Goddess Sadia. "You don't have the leeway to send me home because you need to focus on returning this zombie-blighted world back to normal. But, at the same time, that also means you will have plenty of leeway once you get the world back in order. Doesn't this mean you'll have spare energy to send me back and forth between worlds once everything is done and settled?"

"Y-You caught on to that part?"

"Mwhahaha!" I cackle.

I spoke confidently, but the truth is that Pino casually tipped me off this morning before I'd left the castle. Thanks, Pino!

"Nevertheless, as I told your knight, transporting people between worlds is taboo—"

"The woman who broke the taboo and ripped me from the comfort of my own bed to clean up her mess has little right to care about taboos when it's convenient for her. Don't you think so too, Goddess?"

"Ack."

"Besides, you already broke it once to bring me here. You'd do it again to send me back. What's a few more times?"

"Y-Your logic sounds like a repeat offender's..."

She put me through hell and nearly cost me my life several times. This is a small price to ask in return.

"I won't be able to send you and bring you back often. It takes a lot of my power, even when I am in tip-top shape."

"Being able to make the trip is enough for me."

## Another World's Zombie Apocalypse Is Not My Problem!

"I do not know how much time it will take for the world to reorder itself. Are you still okay with waiting?"

"Yes, I've already made up my mind."

"You sound firm in your resolve. Very well, then. However, under one condition."

I didn't think she'd have a condition. I instinctively prepare myself for the worst possible demand that she'd ask in return for what I want.

"The piece of my power that currently resides in you—I had originally planned on taking it back when I sent you home, but…I shall leave it in your care."

"Um, should I take that to mean you want me to help you purify the world?"

"It helps that you are quick on the uptake."

Oh, that's all she wants? I'm internally relieved by her simple request.

"Okay."

"That was…a quick decision."

"Well, that's what I planned to do all along anyway."

If Goddess Sadia hadn't requested it first, I would have asked her to let me help. It ties into what I want to do with my life.

Goddess Sadia smiles softly. "As I thought, I was correct to choose you."

"I'm going to make full use of my goddess perks!" I make a joke of it, getting a giggle out of Goddess Sadia.

Yesterday, she told me my heart is closest to hers in the multiverse, and I kind of get why now. She's not a complete stranger. There's a familiarity between us that makes me think that way.

"I shall be going, then."

Not to any particular place—she is going to become a part of the world in order to maintain it.

"Until we meet again."

"Yes. Until the day the world is right again."

With those final words, Goddess Sadia's body flashes. By the time the light settles, she's no longer there.

"She left," Lex says.

"…Yeah."

For a time, we stare at where Goddess Sadia had been standing. Even if her disappearance is the right thing, it is still lonely to watch a person vanish before your eyes.

That being said, we can't stay here forever. Plus, I'm dying to do something right now.

"Okay, shall we go home? To our country!"

# ◆Epilogue: In a Wonderful World

**THE** main street from the capital city to the castle is jam-packed with people. Since coming to this world, I have never seen so many living humans in one place before. When the capital was overrun by zombies, things were pretty crowded too, but even more people are in the city now.

"I'm amazed by how many people are here…"

"This is everyone who regained their humanity thanks to you, Big Sister."

"It's moving when you put it that way, but I think I'm more shocked than anything."

I'm walking down the main street holding hands with Cia. At our sides are Lex, Sir Julian, and Sir Kurt. A dozen or so more knights are marching around us, eliminating the fear of being trampled by the crowds.

A festival that began at noon is being held to celebrate successfully vanquishing the Dark Djinn. Despite being called a festival, it's nothing like the ones I know of. A few street stalls are set up here and there selling food, but circumstances being what they are, it's nothing too extravagant. The portions aren't big either. Even so, some people have set up shop for others to enjoy themselves, as everyone's brimming with excitement.

"Everyone seems like they're having a good time."

"Optimism is one of the virtues of Grantz's citizens."

"I'm sure the kingdom will be rebuilt in no time if the people keep their spirits up."

"Certainly! I also want to do everything in my power as princess to help!"

Time flies, as they say, and a month has passed since Goddess Sadia left.

Some sectors of the city are still in disrepair, but their restoration is steadily progressing. As for food supplies, my saliva is needed to hold us over for the time being, but it's anticipated I'll be out of that business once they can start growing and harvesting stabilized crops. I don't plan to pester them into rushing, but I sure hope they go as fast as they possibly can in order for me to salvage my dignity.

"Holy Priestess!"

Several people waiting on the side of the street suddenly call out to me.

"Thank you very much for always blessing us with delicious water…!"

"We are able to continue farming thanks to you, Holy Priestess!"

Words of gratitude come from many people along the street, not just them. They make such a big deal out of it that my reaction of "Th-Thanks" sounds kind of flat in return, but it leaves me feeling pretty good about myself.

Lex speaks to me over my shoulder while I wave to the people of Grantz. "You seem very at home in your role as priestess now."

"It's hard not to get used to it after people have been saying it to me for months…"

Shortly after parting ways with Goddess Sadia, I had an audience with the recovered king and queen…where they showered me with overwhelming thanks for saving Grantz Kingdom from the zombie apocalypse. As if their gratitude alone wasn't enough, they even announced they officially recognized me as the holy priestess.

Of course, I begged and pleaded with them not to at first, but after Pino advised me that "you'll be able to move around more freely with Holy Priestess as your title," I gave in. After all, I wholeheartedly agreed with him that having a title to my name would grant me a level of freedom that would make things easier as I help Grantz Kingdom recover.

"Oh? Is that Boss Lady there?!" someone exclaims. I follow the direction of that lively voice to Rosso. He's standing behind a large

## Another World's Zombie Apocalypse Is Not My Problem!

wooden table stacked with loaves of bread.

"Rosso? You opened a street stall?"

"Seemed like the right occasion to make a big score. Hehe."

"Brother! Don't say things that cause misunderstandings!" a girl standing beside Rosso scolds. She appears slightly older than Cia. Her shoulder-length red hair and big round eyes are striking.

"My bad. I haven't introduced ya yet. This here is my kid sister, Maybelle."

"I-It is a pleasure to meet you, Priestess! Thank you for looking after my big brother all the time." She must be pretty panicked, because she bows so low she smacks her forehead against the table. She seems like a klutz. Her eyes water from embarrassment and pain. Is there any way I can distract her from it?

"Oh, right. The bread you gave me the other day was delicious!"

"Was it really?! Thank you! Thank yo—"

KLONK! She smacks her forehead again. Rosso roars with laughter as he watches Maybelle clamp her hands over her forehead and whimper.

"This girl has been your admirer ever since she heard about you from me, Boss Lady."

"H-Hey! Rosso! Don't..."

I thought she was going to punch Rosso, but instead she glances at me and bashfully lowers her gaze... Rosso was telling the truth, then.

"So, what did you tell her about me?" I ask.

"All 'bout your awesome open-handed slaps, of course. How you purify incomin' zombies by slapping 'em so hard they catch air. Nobody normal is capable of pullin' somethin' like that off. I seriously respect you!"

"A-Ahaha... Hey, Maybelle? Just so you know, Rosso's stories are exaggerated. I'm much gentler with my touch than that, okay?"

"B-But I caught some real air from your slap too!"

Who would have thought she's experienced it for herself! I need to be more careful with how hard I hit in the future.

A commotion rises behind me as I'm reflecting on my actions.

"MiZUhaaaa!"

"Oh gosh, he's here." It's annoying that I know who that is now without needing to check. With one cheek twitching, I ask Rosso, "Is it who I think it is?"

"Yep. It's that guy," Rosso tells me, shrugging.

Resigned to my fate, I look over my shoulder at who I expected to find there—Keith. The knights are preventing him from coming any closer, but he's struggling against them while holding up a bouquet.

"You are going to accept my love for sure today!"

"...You never learn, do you?"

"How could I when it is destined for you to marry me in the end?!"

Ever since the Dark Djinn was vanquished, Keith proposes once every two days or so. I give him credit for holding to his guns and not giving up yet.

I'm shooting him a frosty glare when Cia questions me with an utterly disgusted face: "Is that true, Big Sister?"

"No, no, it is not. Please don't believe this man's delusions."

"Has he been bothering you?"

"Yeah. A whole lot."

"All right. Sir Julian. Sir Kurt."

At Cia's orders, Sir Julian and Sir Kurt firmly seize Keith's arms.

"Wh-What are you doing?!"

"Following Her Highness's orders. Please come quietly."

"Do you think you can get away with treating me like this?! Dammit! Unhand me! MiZUha! MiZUhaaa!"

Keith is callously dragged out of sight. I can hear him howling my name for a while even after he's gone. I really wish he'd stop embarrassing me this way.

"Let us be on our way, Big Sister." Cia tugs on my hand, smiling ear to ear. My little secret is that I got chills from her dismissive behavior toward Keith.

We parade through the capital city for some time after that. I eat various types of food and talk to all different people. To be blunt, the entertainment provided doesn't vary, but they bring a smile to my face wherever I go.

After arriving at the end of the main street, Cia returns to the castle exhausted from all the walking, leaving me and Lex alone. I climb the outer wall and sit dangling my legs off the ledge facing the city. Beneath the darkening sky, people can be seen here and there, enjoying the final hurrah of the festivities in the city.

"Do you not regret it, m'lady?"

## Another World's Zombie Apocalypse Is Not My Problem!

"Hmm? Regret what?"

I know what Lex is trying to ask.

"Well, that is to say..."

"I don't regret it," I say, answering his original question while kicking my legs. "I mean, sure there are tons of things I'm upset I haven't gotten used to yet. But there is so much more I have gained from this world."

Like the strong connection between people as they work toward rebuilding Grantz. There might be places where you can find that back on my world too, but to me, that place is here, not there. I feel like I can grow as a person in this world.

"Why? Do I look like I regret it to you, Lex?"

"...You look like you are having the time of your life."

"Don't I?" I rise to my feet and dust the dirt off my butt with both hands. I spin around until I'm facing Lex. "Life would be perfect if we could just do something about that foul zombie stench."

"I cannot do anything to help you there, but...I swear I will protect you from zombies."

"Just from zombies?"

"No. I will protect you from anything that means you harm, Lady Mizuha."

It's so not fair that he can say embarrassing lines like that without blushing. I've got my hands full trying to hide my embarrassment behind my laughter. Suddenly, a warm, ticklish feeling fills my chest. I place my hand over my heart. The number-one reason why I chose to stay is...a frustrating one, so I decided to keep it to myself for the time being.

A scream suddenly rips through the air. It's easy to find where it came from. People are running chaotically, trying to escape from the main street. A lone zombie is staggering behind them. It's not nighttime yet, so it can't have come over the walls. With all the gates shut, there's only one reason why a zombie could be inside.

"Yeesh! I just did the stupid handshake session yesterday too!"

"Mayhap they arbitrarily assumed they would be fine without it because zombies haven't shown up lately."

"Whatever the case, we have to hurry and purify that zombie! Let's go, Lex!"

"Yes, m'lady!"

I race down the staircase behind Lex. I'm so used to it that a single zombie during the day isn't the least bit scary. But that's only because of the broad, reliable back in front of me.

"Hey, Lex! I'm counting on you from now on!"

"What brought that up out of the blue?!"

"I just felt like saying it right now!"

Lex looks over his shoulder as he continues running. "Of course you can count on me, for I am your knight, Lady Mizuha!"

I can't help laughing at his expected response. He has guts, being able to say that with a straight face. But it's because he is like this that I can move forward without fear. I know that won't change in the future either. Even in a post-apocalyptic world overrun by zombies.

"Yeah, I'm depending on you!"

**Another World's Zombie Apocalypse Is Not My Problem!**

## ◆After Story

"**LADY** Mizuha! Happy birthday!"

"Happy birthday! Priestess Mizuha!"

"MiZUha! Happy birthday to you!"

I'm taking a leisurely ride in a carriage down the main street of Grantz's capital, bordered on all sides by crowds of people.

Bands perform catchy songs around the carriage. Grantz Kingdom's knights march in perfect step to the beat. What seems like a parade is being held entirely in my honor. Wearing a light-blue gown that doesn't suit me hasn't gone to my head and made me think this is all for me—it's undeniably true that this parade is for me.

"I'm so glad we made it in time," Cia says, sighing with relief where she sits beside me.

Cia asked me about my birthday the day before yesterday. I've had my hands full with the zombie apocalypse ever since I was launched from my bed into this world, and it's not like there's a calendar around. Because of that, I had entirely forgotten about my birthday until she asked, but since she did, I counted how many days had passed since being hurled here and realized that today is my birthday.

Once I told Cia that, it was decided on the spot that a birthday celebration was to be held for me, and things moved rapidly from there. It's mostly thanks to Cia's gusto, but the king and queen were surprisingly all for it, which is why it happened so fast. When they set their minds to it, this family can make anything absurd happen. This was the moment I worried about the future of Grantz Kingdom for the millionth time.

"Uh, but don't you think this is going overboard...? I would've been happier with something small."

"You are the holy priestess who saved our kingdom, Big Sister. Your birth should be celebrated on scale with your great deeds."

Cia says that like it's only natural, but this parade is hard to accept as someone who was just a normal high school girl up until recently. Lex rides close to the carriage on Vianta, probably because I'm still frowning.

"Please put your mind at ease, m'lady. No one was compelled to be here. The soldiers gladly volunteered, and the citizens came because they wanted to."

I certainly don't see anyone who looks unhappy to be here. They are all cheering for me with broad smiles.

"Lady Mizuha, thank you for everything you do!"

"I am only alive today thanks to you, Priestess Mizuha!"

"MiZUha! I've awoken to love thanks to you!"

Countless words of gratitude, with the occasional weird comments thrown in, are showered on me from the crowd. The powers I have as priestess are not my own, but I've been through lots of horrible, scary, stinky...and stinkier experiences. That's why their gratitude feels like they are recognizing what I endured for them, and that honestly makes me happy.

"W-Well...I can accept that, then." I sheepishly look away from Lex, sweeping my gaze over the crowd instead.

A little over a month has passed since I met with Goddess Sadia. Many areas still haven't been repaired yet, but the rebuilding process is proceeding quickly thanks to everyone's hard work.

If we keep this up, it won't be long before I can see how beautiful the capital once— No, how much more amazing the capital will become than it ever was before.

I'm going to work even harder so as not to lose out to the others, because this is my problem now!

"**I'M** exhausted..." I dive face-first into my bed after the birthday festivities are over. I didn't do an intense workout or use my powers;

## Another World's Zombie Apocalypse Is Not My Problem!

this is simply a case of mental fatigue from being the center of a lot of attention.

Fortunately, they didn't want me to give a speech. In my world, people who are being celebrated during a big event like this would almost always be expected to give some kind of speech. Would they have requested one if this world had some sort of PA system? Makes me shudder just thinking about it. I'm not proud of it, but I'm the type who got nervous when the teacher called on me in class. I'm confident I'd either faint or throw up if I had to speak in front of an ocean of people.

I suddenly hear someone rapping on my door. "Lady Mizuha," Lex calls from the corridor. "I apologize for bothering you when you are tired, but may I have a minute of your time?"

"Did something happen? N-Not another zombie, is it?"

"No. Several visitors are here with gifts for you."

We live in a city just recently liberated from zombies, with their threat always around the corner. Presents had completely slipped my mind to the point that I'm left blinking at the door. I feel guilty receiving gifts, but on the other hand, if you remove the part about my having priestess powers, this is my birthday. Excitement wells up inside me at the prospect of getting presents.

I hastily fix my sitting posture and respond to Lex. "O-Okay. You can let them in now."

"I shall let them inside in order, then."

And so, he allows Rosso into my bedchamber first. Rosso hands me a sparkling, glistening bracelet. I can tell at a glance that it's expensive, with diamonds the size of the tip of my pinkie finger decorating it.

"Wow! It's gorgeous. But how did you afford it?"

"It's obviously somethin' I prepared for you, Boss Lady."

"Are there any jewelry shops open yet? You didn't steal it, did you?"

"Whoops," Rosso groans, pulling a clearly guilty face the second I ask. His reaction says it all. "But I don't do it anymore…"

"It's still bad if you did it before. Gifting someone with stolen goods is low. And for that matter, you need to return the things you stole before. I'm going to have Lex look into whether you've returned everything or not."

"B-Boss Ladyyyy!"

This is the correct way to deal with him. Honestly, it wouldn't be strange if he wound up in jail for all his crimes. I know he's a good guy deep down, but I can't turn a blind eye on his compulsive thievery.

Iris comes next, after my first gift giver started off the occasion by making me sigh. I get a bad feeling about her present the second she enters my room because she's carrying something the length and size of her full wingspan spread from hand to hand, including the shoulders. I don't know what it is definitively because it's covered by a cloth, but it can be only *that*.

Iris yanks the cloth off with pomp, a smile bursting onto her face. "This is the newest goddess statue!"

"I told you to stop making those! Hold on, why does that look like the gown I wore today…?"

"I researched the design beforehand and rushed to finish it!"

"It's scary how well prepared you are."

Whether I want this thing or not, it's still a carved statue of me. Destroying it would be unsettling, so I accept—or rather, confiscate—the statue, but I honestly don't know what to do with it.

A surprising person visits me after Iris—Sir Oden, the captain of Grantz Kingdom's Royal Knights and the man befitting of the name "the Reigning King of Charges."

"Grantz—nay, the world—should prioritize your life above all else, Lady Mizuha. Therefore, I would like to present you with this shield."

He hands me a metal shield twice my size. This shield would definitely be capable of blocking charging zombies without breaking. However…

"Um, it takes all my strength just to hold it up…"

"Then you must begin training. Gahaha!" Sir Oden lets out a hearty laugh. Even if I train hard, this shield won't work with my physique. But I keep my mouth shut since I fear him countering my objections with "Then you have no choice but to put your back into it, lass!"

After Lex helps me move the shield aside, I welcome my next visitor.

"MiZUha! Today for sure you will wear this engagement ring—"

"Send him home."

The door shuts in Keith's face. I can hear his grating voice fussing in the corridor for a while before it's gradually dragged away. The soldiers must have escorted him outside of the castle for me.

Sheer exhaustion crushes down on me. Heaving the loudest sigh, I

# Another World's Zombie Apocalypse Is Not My Problem!

slump onto my bed.

"I'm happy they gave me presents, but…I have little to say about it… Yeah…"

I don't want to say anything rude when they gave me those gifts with good intentions. But not only are they all things I don't know how to use, I'm worried about where to even put them. Frankly speaking, I wasn't happy about any of it.

"H-Hey, Lex? No one else is coming with presents, right?"

"I don't believe so. Lord Rowadan was the last I saw in line."

"I-I see. Hmm."

"Is something the matter?"

"Nothing is the matter," I reply half-heartedly, glancing at and away from Lex several times. He frowns and cocks his head.

I actually want to ask him if he has a gift for me. But it's too embarrassing for me to bring it up first. As I'm impatiently twitching and twiddling my thumbs, Lex works up the nerve to speak.

"Actually…I also prepared a present for you. Will you accept it?"

"Wha-? Y-You did?" I can't tell him I've been super looking forward to what he got me. "Of course, I will accept anything that's within acceptable bounds. As long as it's not stolen goods, a creepy statue of me, or a shield so big I'll be squashed under it."

"Please rest assured that it is nothing special like what the others gave you. Please wait just a moment." Lex leaves the bedchamber temporarily to retrieve the present he left elsewhere. He comes back a short time later with a flower growing out of a flowerpot small enough for me to hold in both hands.

"Oh, wow! This is so cute…!"

The flower petals are on the petite side and possess the same glamorousness as a fancy gown. Just like the people who brought me gifts earlier, Lex hasn't lost his weirdo image, so I had prepared myself for something strange to come, making this an unexpected surprise. A good surprise, of course.

"Say, what is this flower called?"

"Del… Delphi… My apologizes, I forgot the full name."

"Someone's unprepared! But I love it because light blue is my favorite color."

"You once told Master Pino the meaning of your name, so I used that for reference."

I had once mentioned to Pino in passing that my name means "light-blue flower." Apparently, Lex remembered that conversation. For the guy who normally has his head in the clouds, he's uncannily a smooth operator when it comes to these things.

"Allow me to say it once again. A very happy birthday to you, Lady Mizuha," Lex says, smiling gently at me from the other side of the light-blue flowers.

He told me this wasn't a special gift, but to me, this is the most special gift of all.

"Thank you…Lex."

Making another world's zombie apocalypse my problem wasn't such a bad idea after all.

**Another World's Zombie Apocalypse Is Not My Problem!**

## ◆Afterword

**HELLO,** Haru Yayari here. This is likely—or rather, unquestionably—the first time we have met.

Now then, I really wonder what I should write. I'm actively putting out light novels and children's books in Japan, but this is the first time I'm being published abroad. You probably can't tell from the text alone, but I'm very nervous.

That being said, I'm also excited. After all, this is a rare opportunity for me to write with readers abroad in mind, instead of my usual afterwords written specifically to Japanese readers. This is a valuable experience. While our time together is short, I would like to fully enjoy this precious time talking with you.

Okay, okay, time to wrap up the talk about me and touch on this novel. First of all, I want to tell you about the clichéd series of events that led to this story's creation. Not that there's a particularly big reason for it.

In Japan, stories about being transported or reincarnated into another world are all the craze. Some of the initial frenzy has cooled down now, but there are still plenty of authors coming up with various scenarios and giving birth to new stories by the day.

As one of those authors, I struck upon the idea to drop a high school girl into a world crawling with zombies. I thought this scenario wouldn't overlap with other authors and would make for an entertaining story.

At the time, I let that inspiration direct my pen wherever it wanted to go… Thinking back on it now, that led to the heroine being dumped into a pretty cruel situation. That's exactly what makes it interesting, but I do want to apologize to her.

As for why zombie tropes are a key element to the story, it's definitely because I often play zombie games. However, right off the bat, I decided I didn't want to include extremely gory or grotesque scenes that are common in zombie games, such as blowing heads off.

My eccentric personality played a big part in my desire to create something different, but it also came from the simple desire to make something fun. Zombies still have a very negative image in society. I thought adding in comedy elements would bring out an entertainment factor different from other stories. The result is what you have all already experienced.

On that note, I can say this only after having completed the story, but it's our little secret that I created one too many crazy characters, which made the story livelier than I had initially planned. Thanks to them, I was able to enjoy myself while writing, so I'm grateful to those characters.

…Whoops! Whenever I talk about my stories, I feel as if I can go on forever, so I would like to take this time to thank the people involved in publishing this story.

Thank you to everyone at Cross Infinite World for granting me this wonderful opportunity. Thanks also to those who assisted in the publication. Most of all, my heartfelt gratitude goes out to those of you who took the time to read this book.

I pray that if you ever find yourself turned into a zombie, you will be purified right away by the priestess's open-handed slap. Until we meet again.

## LITTLE PRINCESS IN FAIRY FOREST
**STORY BY: TSUBAKI TOKINO**
**ILLUSTRATION BY: TAKASHI KONNO**
*STANDALONE | OUT NOW*

Join Princess Lala and Sir Gideon as they flee for their lives from the traitor who killed the royal family and wants to wed Lala! Gideon is willing to do anything to protect his princess, even if it means engaging the mighty dragons in combat! Tsubaki Tokino's fairy tale inspired Little Princess in Fairy Forest!

## THE WEREWOLF COUNT AND THE TRICKSTER TAILOR
**STORY BY: YURUKA MORISAKI**
**ILLUSTRATION BY: TSUKITO**
*VOL. 1 | OUT NOW*

"I don't care if you are a man, let me court you."
Rock's whole life is shaken when a werewolf shows up at her shop in the middle of the night...asking for more than just clothes!

## THE ECCENTRIC MASTER AND THE FAKE LOVER!
**STORY BY: ROKA SAYUKI**
**ILLUSTRATION BY: ITARU**
*VOL. 1 OUT NOW*

Yanked into another world full of dangerous magic and parasitic plants, Nichika does the one thing she can to survive: become the apprentice to an eccentric witch!

## THE CHAMPIONS OF JUSTICE AND THE SUPREME RULER OF EVIL
**STORY BY: KAEDE KIKYOU**
**ILLUSTRATION BY: TOBARI**
*STANDALONE | OUT NOW*

Mia's a supervillain bent on world domination who lacks tact in enacting her evil schemes! Will the lazy superheroes be able to stop her?

## BEAST † BLOOD
**STORY BY: SATO FUMINO**
**ILLUSTRATION BY: AKIRA EGAWA**
*VOL. 1 OUT NOW*

Biotech Scientist Euphemia's world suddenly gets flipped upside down when her sister hires a sexy alien mercenary to be her bodyguard!

## THE CURSED PRINCESS AND THE LUCKY KNIGHT
**STORY BY: UTA NARUSAWA**
**ILLUSTRATION BY: TAKASHI KIRIYA**
*STANDALONE | OUT NOW*

Orphan Sonia leaves the abbey only to be haunted by her own castle! Is an arranged marriage to a knight her only salvation from the family curse?

Made in the USA
Coppell, TX
18 January 2022

71798545R00134